MathFlare

Name: _______________________

Class: ___________

Teacher: _______________________

Introduction

As parents and educators, we recognize the pivotal role mathematics plays in shaping a child's academic journey and future success. Yet, the path to mathematical proficiency can often seem daunting, fraught with challenges and complexities. That's where the transformative power of MathFlare Workbooks shine through, illuminating the way forward with clarity, precision, and purpose.

Introducing MathFlare Workbooks – a beacon of guidance, a testament to excellence, and a catalyst for achievement. Crafted with meticulous care and expertise, MathFlare Workbooks stand as paragons of educational excellence, designed to nurture young minds, ignite a passion for learning, and develop a deep-rooted understanding of mathematical concepts.

Picture this: your child eagerly delves into the pages of Mathflare Workbook, greeted by a step-by-step guide illuminated with vivid examples that demystify complex mathematical concepts. With each turn of the page, they embark on a journey of discovery, encountering thoughtfully curated practice questions that reinforce learning and hone problem-solving skills. And when they unveil the answers to those very questions, a sense of accomplishment blossoms within them – a tangible reward for their hard work and dedication.

But MathFlare Workbooks are more than just tools for learning; they are pathways to comprehension, fostering a deep-seated understanding of mathematical concepts through a sequential, logical flow. From fundamental principles to advanced problem-solving strategies, every chapter builds upon the last, ensuring a robust foundation upon which future knowledge can be constructed.

As parents, we yearn for nothing more than to see our children thrive, to witness the spark of inspiration ignited within them as they conquer academic challenges with confidence and poise. MathFlare Workbooks serve as partners in this noble endeavor, offering not just practice questions, but the keys to unlocking a world of opportunity.

And for teachers, MathFlare Workbooks stand as invaluable allies in the quest to cultivate mathematical proficiency in the classroom. With answers readily available, instructors can focus on guiding and nurturing their students, confident in the knowledge that MathFlare Workbooks provide a solid framework upon which to build.

In the pages of MathFlare Workbooks, we find not just the promise of academic excellence, but the seeds of a brighter tomorrow. So let us embrace the power of mathematics, let us champion the journey of learning, and let us pave the way for a generation of young minds poised to shape the world. With MathFlare Workbooks as our guide, the possibilities are infinite, and the future, bright.

Table of Contents

MathFlare
MATH
WORKBOOK
Grade 2
Step by Step Guide
and Essential Practice
with Answers
Addition
Subtraction
Multiplication
Place Value and
Expanded
Notations
Geometry
MathFlare Publishing

MathFlare
MATH
WORKBOOK
Grade 2-3
Step by Step Guide
and Essential Practice
with Answers
Addition
Subtraction
Multiplication
and Division
Place Value and
Expanded
Notations
Geometry
MathFlare Publishing

MathFlare
MATH
WORKBOOK
Grade 3
Step by Step Guide
and Essential Practice
with Answers
Multiplication
and Division
Decimals
Place Value and
Expanded
Notations
Fractions
and Geometry
MathFlare Publishing

MathFlare
MATH
WORKBOOK
Grade 1
Step by Step Guide
and Essential Practice
with Answers
Counting and
Numbers
Addition and
Subtraction
Place Value and
Expanded
Notations
Understanding
Time
MathFlare Publishing

MathFlare
MATH
WORKBOOK
Grade 1-2
Step by Step Guide
and Essential Practice
with Answers
Counting and
Numbers
Addition and
Subtraction
Place Value and
Expanded
Notations
Understanding
Time
MathFlare Publishing

MathFlare
MATH
WORKBOOK
Grade 3-4
Step by Step Guide
and Essential Practice
with Answers
Addition
Subtraction
Multiplication
Division
Place Value and
Expanded
Notations
Fractions
and Geometry
MathFlare Publishing

MathFlare
MATH
WORKBOOK
Grade 4
Step by Step Guide
and Essential Practice
with Answers
Addition
Subtraction
Multiplication
Division
Place Value and
Expanded
Notations
Fractions
and Geometry
MathFlare Publishing

MathFlare
MATH
WORKBOOK
Grade 4-5
Step by Step Guide
and Essential Practice
with Answers
Multiplication
Division
Place Value and
Expanded
Notations
Fractions
and Geometry
Unit
Conversion
MathFlare Publishing

MathFlare
MATH WORKBOOK
5
Step by Step Guide and Essential Practice with Answers
Multiplication Division
Place Value and Expanded Notations
Fractions and Geometry
Unit Conversion
MathFlare Publishing

MathFlare
MATH WORKBOOK
5-6
Step by Step Guide and Essential Practice with Answers
Multiplication Division
Place Value and Expanded Notations
Fractions and Geometry
Units and Statistics
MathFlare Publishing

MathFlare
MATH WORKBOOK
6
Step by Step Guide and Essential Practice with Answers
Integers and Statistics
Arithmetic and Pre-Algebra
Fractions and Geometry
Ratio and Percentage
MathFlare Publishing

MathFlare
MATH WORKBOOK
6-7
Step by Step Guide and Essential Practice with Answers
Arithmetic and Pre-Algebra
Ratio, Percent Proportion
Geometry
Statistics
MathFlare Publishing

MathFlare
MATH WORKBOOK
7
Step by Step Guide and Essential Practice with Answers
Pre-Algebra
Ratio, Percent Proportion
Geometry
Statistics
MathFlare Publishing

MathFlare
MATH WORKBOOK
7-8
Step by Step Guide and Essential Practice with Answers
Pre-Algebra
Ratio, Percent Proportion
Geometry and Cartesian Plane
Statistics
MathFlare Publishing

MathFlare
MATH WORKBOOK
8-9
Step by Step Guide and Essential Practice with Answers
Pre-Algebra
Ratio, Proportion and Percentage
Linear Equations
Geometry and Cartesian Plane
MathFlare Publishing

MathFlare
MATH WORKBOOK
8
Step by Step Guide and Essential Practice with Answers
Pre-Algebra
Percentage
Linear Equations
Geometry
MathFlare Publishing

Decimals

Adding Decimals

Adding decimals is like adding whole numbers, but we must align the decimal points carefully. For instance, when adding 49.88 and 45.78:

Step 1: Align the decimal points.

$$49.88$$
$$+\ 45.78$$

Step 2: Start adding from the rightmost digit (the ones place) and move to the left.

Add 8 and 8: 8 + 8 = 16. Write down 6 in the ones place and carry over 1 to the tenths place.

$$49.88$$
$$+\ 45.78$$
$$6$$

Step 3: Add the tenths place.

Add 1 (carried over from the previous step), 8, and 7: 1 + 8 + 7 = 16. Write down 6 in the tenths place and carry over 1 to the hundredths place.

$$49.88$$
$$+\ 45.78$$
$$66$$

49.88

+ 45.78

9566

Step 5: Finally, write the sum with the decimal point directly below the decimal points in the original numbers.

49.88

+ 45.78

95.66

Subtracting Decimals

Subtracting decimals follows a process like adding decimals, except instead of adding the numbers, we subtract them.

Let's solve more problems:

176.07	738.71
+ 765.69	- 715.74
941.76	22.97

<u>Multiplying Decimals</u>

Multiplying decimals is a lot like multiplying whole numbers, but we need to be careful about where we put the decimal point in the answer.

Step 1: Start by multiplying the numbers together, just like we do with whole numbers. Ignore the decimals for now.

Step 2: Count how many decimal places there are in the numbers we're multiplying. This will tell us how many decimal places our answer should have.

Step 3: Put the decimal point in the answer by starting from the right side of the number. Move the decimal point to the left as many places as there are in the total number of decimal places.

For example, let's multiply 4.5 by 2.5:

Step 1: Multiply the numbers as if they were whole numbers:

$$25 \times 45 = 1125.$$

Step 2: There is one decimal place in 2.5 and one in 4.5, making a total of two decimal places.
Step 3: Starting from the right side of the answer, count two places to the left and put the decimal point there.

So, the final answer is 11.25.

Remember to pay close attention to where the decimal point goes in the answer.

Let's solve a problem:

$$
\begin{array}{r}
22.93 \\
\times \quad 4.69 \\
\hline
+ \quad 20637 \\
+13758 \\
+9172 \\
\hline
=1075417
\end{array}
$$

Rewrite the product with
4 decimal places.
So the answer is 107.5417

Dividing Decimals

Dividing decimals is a lot like dividing whole numbers, but we need to be careful about placement of decimal point in the answer.

Steps to follow:

1. **Set up the division problem:** Write the dividend (the number being divided) and the divisor (the number you're dividing by) as you would in a long division problem.

$$1.7\,\overline{)1.6}$$

2. **Move the decimal:** Move the decimal point to the right in the dividend and divisor by the same number of places.

$$17\overline{)16}$$

3. **Perform the division:** Divide as you would with whole numbers.

$$
\begin{array}{r}
0\,0.9\,4 \\
17\overline{)16} \\
-\,0 \\
\hline
16 \\
-\,0 \\
\hline
16\,0 \\
-15\,3 \\
\hline
7\,0 \\
-6\,8 \\
\hline
2
\end{array}
$$

4. **Place the decimal point:** Place the decimal point in the quotient directly above its position in the dividend.

So, the quotient is 0.94.

Fractions

Fractions represent parts of a whole. They consist of a numerator (the number on top) and a denominator (the number on the bottom).

For example: we have an orange, and we divide it into 5 equal slices. Each slice represents $\frac{1}{5}$ of the orange. Now, if we take 3 of those slices, we have taken $\frac{3}{5}$ of the orange.

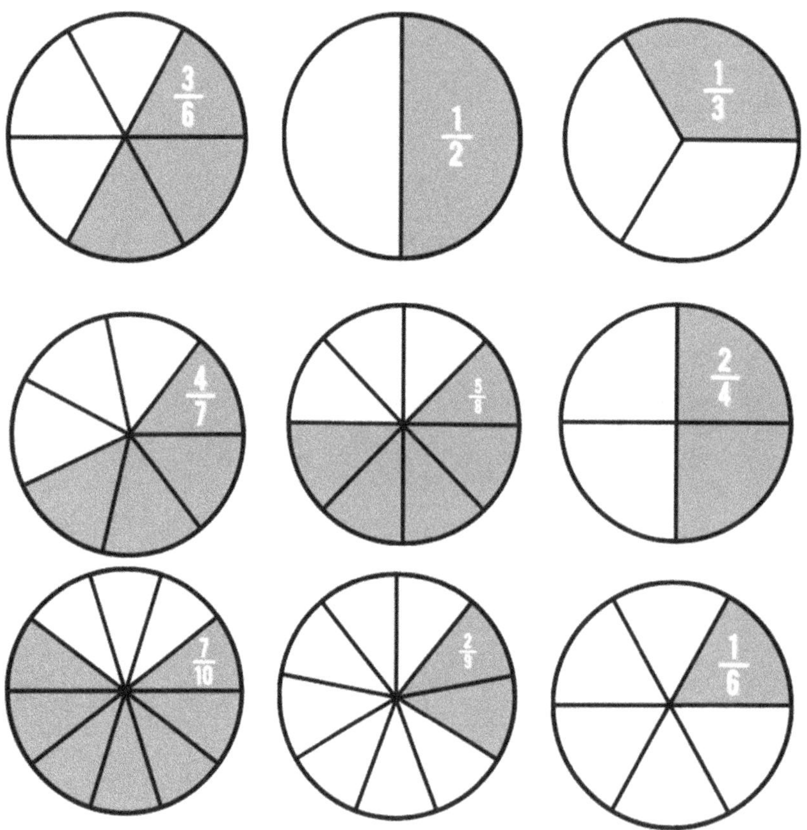

Equivalent Fractions

Equivalent fractions are fractions that represent the same value or part of a whole, even though they may look different.

To find equivalent fractions, you can:

- Multiply or divide both the numerator and denominator by the same nonzero number.
- Simplify fractions to their simplest form.

$\frac{1}{2}$ and $\frac{2}{4}$ are equivalent fractions because if you multiply the numerator and denominator of $\frac{1}{2}$ by 2, you get $\frac{2}{4}$. Similarly, if you divide both the numerator and denominator of $\frac{2}{4}$ by 2, you get $\frac{1}{2}$.

Let's solve a problem:

$$\frac{}{8} = \frac{15}{40}$$

To solve the missing numerator, we can cross multiply.

$$40x = 8 \times 15$$

$$40x = 120$$

$$x = \frac{120}{40} = x = 3$$

$$\frac{3}{8} = \frac{15}{40}$$

Convert Fractions and Decimals

To transform a fraction into a decimal, we divide the numerator by the denominator.

For instance, $\frac{1}{4}$ equals 0.25 because when we divide 1 by 4, we get 0.25.

In certain cases, the resulting decimal repeats infinitely, like $\frac{1}{3}$, which equals 0.3333...

In such instances, we round the decimal to a specific number of decimal places.

Let's solve a problem:

$$\frac{52}{100} = \underline{\ 0.52\ }$$

Least Common Multiple (LCM)

The Lowest Common Multiple (LCM) of two or more numbers is the smallest multiple that is divisible by each of the numbers.

There are several methods to find the LCM; however, we will focus on only two:

Listing Multiples: List the multiples of each number until you find a common multiple. For example:

$$\begin{array}{l l} 8 & \underline{8,\ 16,\ 24,\ 32,\ 40,\ 48,\ 56} \\ 7 & \underline{7,\ 14,\ 21,\ 28,\ 35,\ 42,\ 49,\ 56} \end{array} \text{, LCM} = \underline{56}$$

Division Method: Divide each number with the smallest prime number that divides at least one of the numbers evenly. The product of all the divisors and quotients is the LCM. For example:

$$
\begin{array}{c|cc}
2 & 7 & 8 \\ \hline
2 & 7 & 4 \\ \hline
2 & 7 & 2 \\ \hline
7 & 7 & 1 \\ \hline
  & 1 & 1
\end{array}
$$

$$\text{LCM} = 2 \times 2 \times 2 \times 7 = \underline{56}$$

Both methods have their advantages. For big numbers, using the division way is usually faster. But if we are working with smaller numbers or like seeing patterns, listing multiples might make more sense.

Fractions Multiplication

To multiply fractions, we simply multiply the numerators together to get the new numerator and multiply the denominators together to get the new denominator.

For example, let's multiply: $\dfrac{2}{4} \times \dfrac{1}{4}$

$$\text{Numerator: } 2 \times 1 = 2$$

$$\text{Denominator: } 4 \times 4 = 16$$

$$\text{Therefore, } \dfrac{2}{16}$$

$$\text{we can simplify the resulting fraction: } \dfrac{1}{8}$$

Let's solve a problem:

$$\dfrac{4}{5} \times \dfrac{4}{5} = \dfrac{4 \times 4}{5 \times 5} = \dfrac{16}{25}$$

Fractions Division

To divide fractions, we multiply by the reciprocal of the divisor.

For example, let's divide:

$$\dfrac{6}{8} \div \dfrac{4}{8}$$

$$\dfrac{6}{8} \times \dfrac{8}{4} = \dfrac{48}{32} = \dfrac{3}{2}$$

$$\frac{6}{8} \times \frac{8}{4} = \frac{48}{32} = \frac{3}{2}$$

Fractions Addition Word Problems

Aria spent $\frac{1}{3}$ of her salary on watches and then $\frac{1}{2}$ of the money on food. How much money did she spend?

$$\frac{1}{3} + \frac{1}{2} = \frac{2 \times 1 + 3 \times 1}{3 \times 2} = \frac{2 + 3}{6} = \frac{5}{6} \qquad \text{she spent } \frac{5}{6} \text{ of her money}$$

Fractions Subtraction Word Problems

A container has $\frac{2}{5}$ of a gallon of milk. If $\frac{2}{6}$ of the milk is taken out and put into another container, how much milk is left in the original container in gallons?

$$\frac{2}{5} - \frac{2}{6} = \frac{2 \times 6 + 2 \times 5}{5 \times 6} = \frac{12 - 10}{30} = \frac{2}{30} = \frac{1}{15}$$

there is $\frac{1}{15}$ gallons of milk is left in original container.

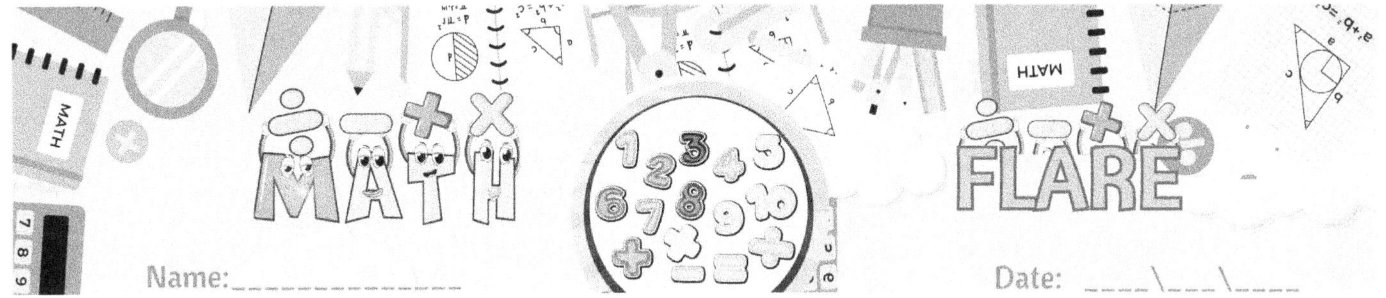

Adding Decimals

Find the sum.

1.   752.039
  + 310.884
  ____

2.   412.271
  + 424.012
  ____

3.   149.579
  + 774.315
  ____

4.   989.806
  + 726.378
  ____

5.   177.738
  + 749.558
  ____

6.   190.653
  + 490.978
  ____

7.   416.221
  + 416.242
  ____

8.   733.666
  + 210.095
  ____

9.   302.681
  + 411.965
  ____

10.   291.866
  + 902.624
  ____

11.   730.471
  + 496.529
  ____

12.   983.336
  + 186.057
  ____

13.   111.269
  + 452.481
  ____

14.   741.571
  + 265.190
  ____

15.   249.184
  + 757.641
  ____

16.   194.431
  + 763.808
  ____

17.   270.379
  + 592.419
  ____

18.   828.409
  + 718.699
  ____

19.   787.800
  + 203.049
  ____

20.   657.747
  + 975.981
  ____

21. 347.616 + 178.774	22. 873.856 + 827.807	23. 219.238 + 640.642	24. 218.302 + 972.794
25. 840.684 + 358.660	26. 361.390 + 828.018	27. 521.634 + 957.835	28. 792.025 + 355.511
29. 327.547 + 326.214	30. 412.743 + 697.097	31. 132.744 + 824.616	32. 577.193 + 420.096
33. 655.127 + 426.844	34. 320.599 + 823.801	35. 587.832 + 114.967	36. 422.294 + 199.632
37. 754.217 + 315.884	38. 655.008 + 651.698	39. 622.672 + 255.529	40. 966.818 + 470.626

41. 334.179 + 768.776	42. 424.505 + 890.524	43. 496.251 + 366.412	44. 342.174 + 312.542
45. 800.392 + 572.898	46. 491.152 + 561.586	47. 790.305 + 960.649	48. 943.237 + 522.998
49. 601.579 + 553.760	50. 272.680 + 792.393	51. 420.043 + 394.500	52. 484.962 + 825.716
53. 936.365 + 261.759	54. 173.801 + 305.750	55. 402.827 + 240.328	56. 732.838 + 172.017
57. 359.395 + 942.115	58. 462.918 + 363.967	59. 500.111 + 686.669	60. 923.844 + 388.715

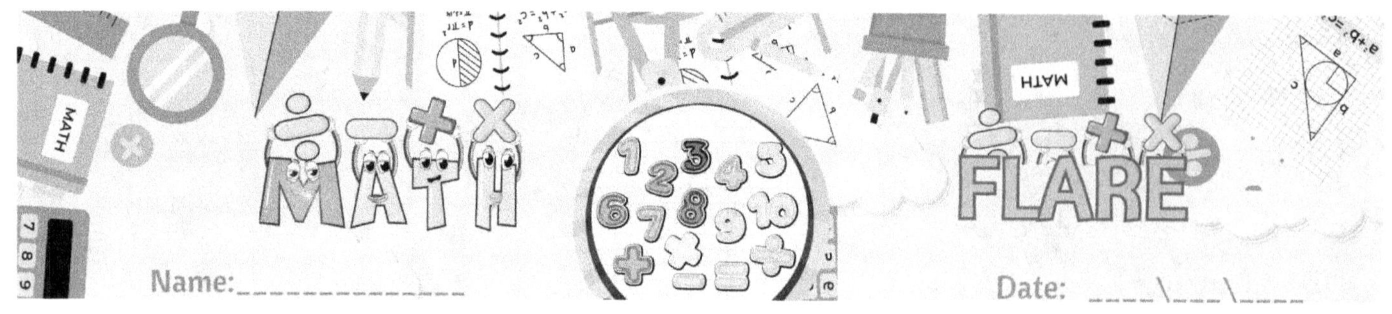

Subtracting Decimals

Find the difference.

61. 224.929 − 990.194	62. 618.269 − 252.920	63. 854.651 − 166.360	64. 604.437 − 853.933
65. 307.293 − 283.706	66. 944.924 − 459.408	67. 893.487 − 998.650	68. 974.712 − 541.251
69. 604.478 − 221.332	70. 994.257 − 987.469	71. 952.807 − 598.384	72. 411.022 − 907.140
73. 524.952 − 760.772	74. 718.632 − 399.633	75. 461.360 − 190.753	76. 827.981 − 863.515
77. 677.202 − 614.801	78. 151.204 − 339.658	79. 598.950 − 803.651	80. 319.840 − 632.697

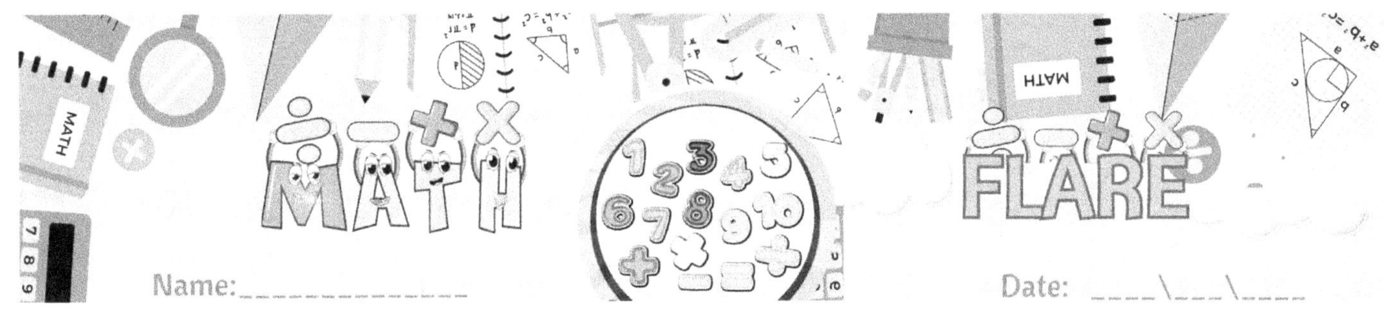

Name:_______________   Date: _______________

81. 617.126 − 428.357	**82.** 733.269 − 604.086	**83.** 714.553 − 854.124	**84.** 114.260 − 296.393
85. 122.509 − 975.757	**86.** 786.818 − 962.965	**87.** 345.471 − 174.129	**88.** 102.195 − 626.442
89. 679.261 − 710.987	**90.** 727.982 − 193.803	**91.** 447.734 − 304.753	**92.** 492.649 − 216.519
93. 455.742 − 181.325	**94.** 782.241 − 378.607	**95.** 947.536 − 734.966	**96.** 942.344 − 800.686
97. 901.503 − 461.470	**98.** 470.431 − 624.364	**99.** 865.165 − 806.814	**100.** 292.667 − 670.695

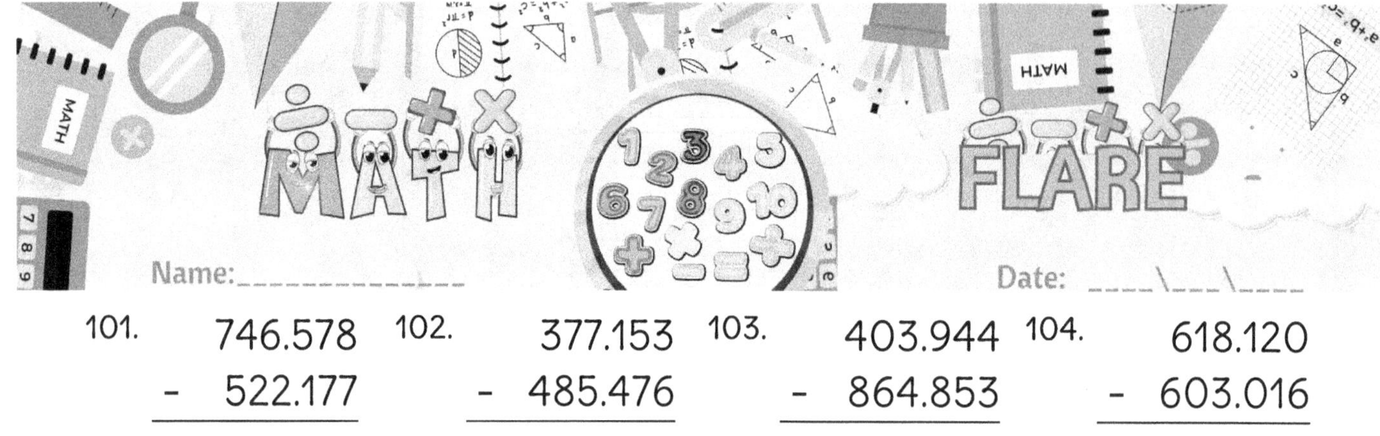

101. 746.578 − 522.177	102. 377.153 − 485.476	103. 403.944 − 864.853	104. 618.120 − 603.016
105. 612.658 − 524.666	106. 660.420 − 887.822	107. 175.740 − 226.015	108. 285.016 − 412.321
109. 935.740 − 616.687	110. 248.394 − 633.166	111. 171.958 − 735.560	112. 348.875 − 387.450
113. 133.500 − 985.972	114. 161.548 − 883.885	115. 703.704 − 477.740	116. 761.329 − 872.299
117. 518.380 − 157.224	118. 447.233 − 925.431	119. 927.620 − 107.134	120. 812.585 − 590.763

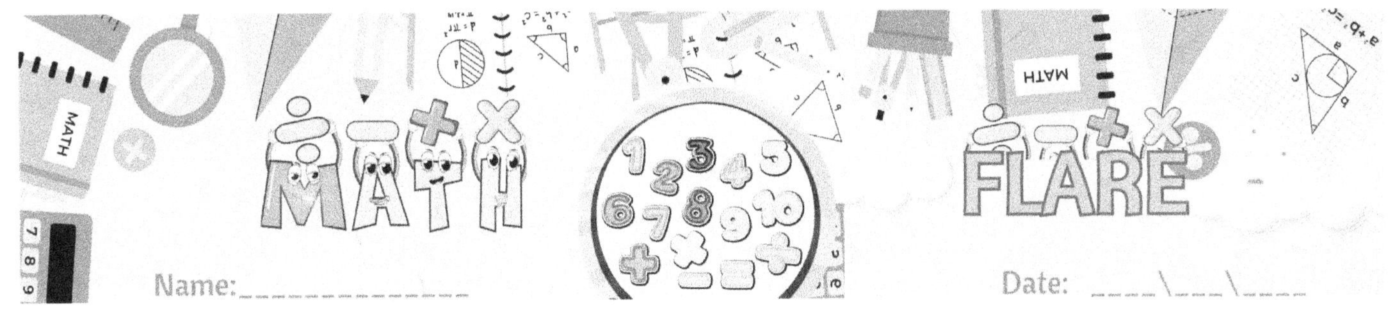

Multiplying Decimals
Find the product.

121.
$$50.82 \times 8.24$$

122.
$$29.57 \times 9.34$$

123.
$$21.70 \times 7.19$$

124.
$$13.22 \times 5.84$$

125.
$$92.16 \times 8.13$$

126.
$$14.93 \times 2.69$$

127.
$$20.08 \times 4.38$$

128.
$$94.10 \times 1.54$$

129.
$$82.80 \times 6.85$$

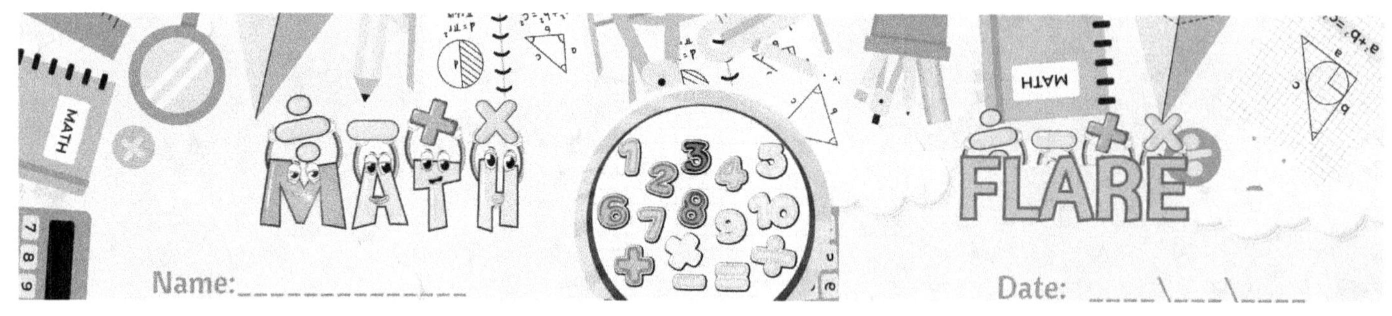

130. 32.21 × 1.94	131. 80.74 × 6.11	132. 36.13 × 6.36
133. 79.33 × 8.16	134. 12.80 × 2.26	135. 85.39 × 9.29
136. 30.39 × 9.04	137. 38.74 × 8.29	138. 89.85 × 6.91

139.
$$\begin{array}{r} 85.89 \\ \times\ \ 2.98 \\ \hline \end{array}$$

140.
$$\begin{array}{r} 94.97 \\ \times\ \ 3.81 \\ \hline \end{array}$$

141.
$$\begin{array}{r} 63.20 \\ \times\ \ 6.59 \\ \hline \end{array}$$

142.
$$\begin{array}{r} 53.76 \\ \times\ \ 9.21 \\ \hline \end{array}$$

143.
$$\begin{array}{r} 99.07 \\ \times\ \ 2.40 \\ \hline \end{array}$$

144.
$$\begin{array}{r} 30.41 \\ \times\ \ 1.27 \\ \hline \end{array}$$

145.
$$\begin{array}{r} 14.59 \\ \times\ \ 2.30 \\ \hline \end{array}$$

146.
$$\begin{array}{r} 42.26 \\ \times\ \ 9.90 \\ \hline \end{array}$$

147.
$$\begin{array}{r} 60.32 \\ \times\ \ 7.86 \\ \hline \end{array}$$

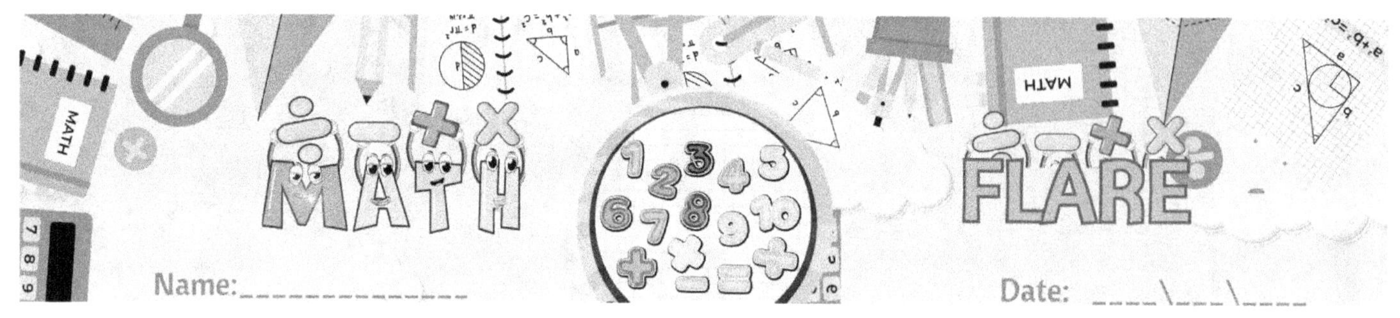

148. 51.50
    × 8.96

149. 56.38
    × 6.58

150. 24.20
    × 4.00

151. 69.14
    × 9.05

152. 73.08
    × 9.91

153. 60.98
    × 2.44

154. 88.20
    × 3.71

155. 53.99
    × 3.49

156. 29.52
    × 6.30

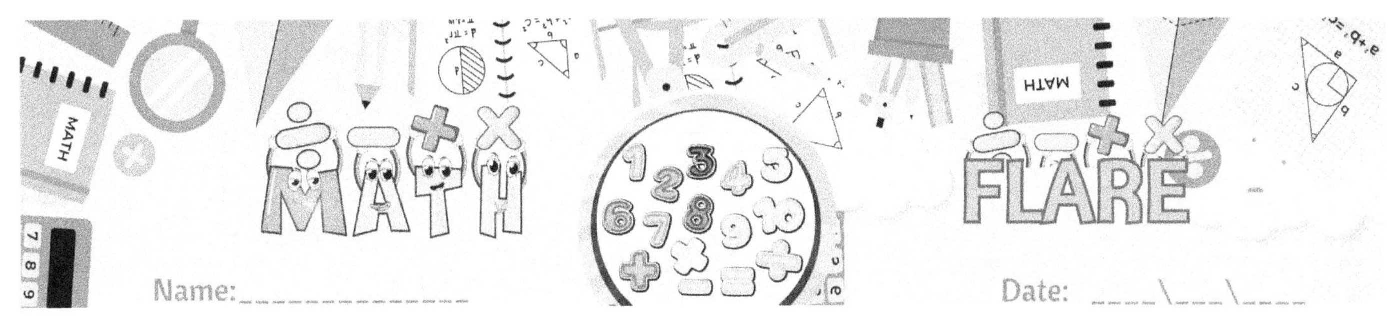

157.
$$\begin{array}{r} 73.53 \\ \times\ 9.40 \\ \hline \end{array}$$

158.
$$\begin{array}{r} 56.24 \\ \times\ 2.48 \\ \hline \end{array}$$

159.
$$\begin{array}{r} 17.39 \\ \times\ 4.39 \\ \hline \end{array}$$

160.
$$\begin{array}{r} 64.61 \\ \times\ 6.53 \\ \hline \end{array}$$

161.
$$\begin{array}{r} 61.29 \\ \times\ 1.01 \\ \hline \end{array}$$

162.
$$\begin{array}{r} 18.02 \\ \times\ 7.23 \\ \hline \end{array}$$

163.
$$\begin{array}{r} 60.69 \\ \times\ 3.13 \\ \hline \end{array}$$

164.
$$\begin{array}{r} 40.14 \\ \times\ 6.00 \\ \hline \end{array}$$

165.
$$\begin{array}{r} 41.43 \\ \times\ 1.02 \\ \hline \end{array}$$

Dividing Decimals
Find the quotient.

166.

$3\overline{)37.3}$

167.

$5\overline{)31.2}$

168.

$5\overline{)95.5}$

169.

$4\overline{)76.1}$

170.

$6\overline{)77.6}$

171.

$3\overline{)48.4}$

172.

$4\overline{)90.5}$

173.

$5\overline{)81.1}$

174.

$5\overline{)73.6}$

175.

$$7 \overline{)28.8}$$

176.

$$9 \overline{)16.6}$$

177.

$$5 \overline{)96.9}$$

178.

$$9 \overline{)86.8}$$

179.

$$6 \overline{)58.4}$$

180.

$$7 \overline{)31.1}$$

181.

$$6 \overline{)17.9}$$

182.

$$9 \overline{)50.0}$$

183.

$$3 \overline{)12.6}$$

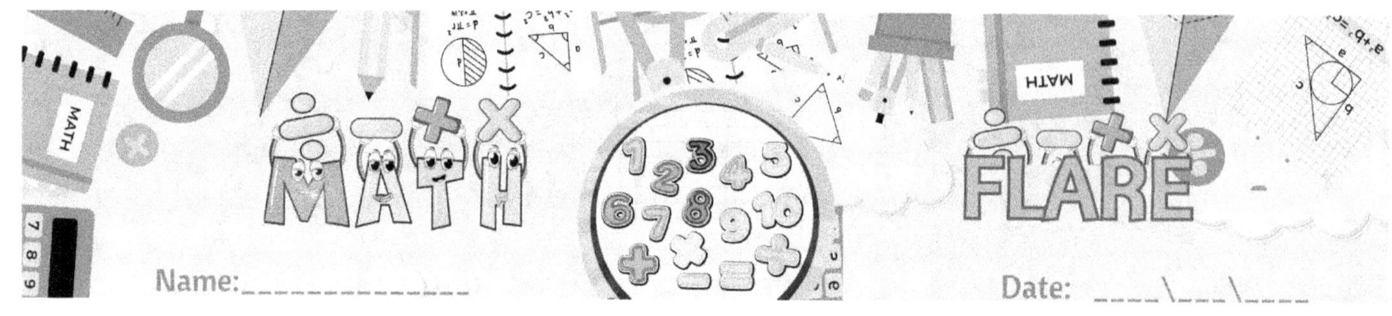

184.

2)27.0

185.

7)11.7

186.

4)88.5

187.

9)84.0

188.

10)47.8

189.

4)77.7

190.

5)97.4

191.

4)77.2

192.

4)47.6

193.

$$4\overline{)42.8}$$

194.

$$8\overline{)36.6}$$

195.

$$1\overline{)65.2}$$

196.

$$2\overline{)87.2}$$

197.

$$2\overline{)20.0}$$

198.

$$9\overline{)51.0}$$

199.

$$2\overline{)75.7}$$

200.

$$6\overline{)39.1}$$

201.

$$6\overline{)28.8}$$

Name:________________   Date: ______________

Equivalent Fractions

202. $\dfrac{1}{8} = \dfrac{5}{} = \dfrac{}{56}$

203. $\dfrac{16}{17} = \dfrac{80}{} = \dfrac{64}{}$

204. $\dfrac{1}{7} = \dfrac{8}{} = \dfrac{}{63}$

205. $\dfrac{2}{9} = \dfrac{}{81} = \dfrac{6}{}$

206. $\dfrac{1}{4} = \dfrac{}{16} = \dfrac{}{12}$

207. $\dfrac{3}{5} = \dfrac{}{45} = \dfrac{21}{}$

208. $\dfrac{11}{12} = \dfrac{22}{} = \dfrac{}{96}$

209. $\dfrac{2}{11} = \dfrac{}{44} = \dfrac{14}{}$

210. $\dfrac{4}{18} = \dfrac{8}{} = \dfrac{}{72}$

211. $\dfrac{1}{2} = \dfrac{7}{} = \dfrac{}{8}$

Name:____________________   Date: ____________

212. $\dfrac{8}{10} = \dfrac{}{60} = \dfrac{72}{}$

213. $\dfrac{1}{14} = \dfrac{}{126} = \dfrac{}{56}$

214. $\dfrac{8}{16} = \dfrac{16}{} = \dfrac{64}{}$

215. $\dfrac{2}{3} = \dfrac{18}{} = \dfrac{8}{}$

216. $\dfrac{4}{13} = \dfrac{}{52} = \dfrac{8}{}$

217. $\dfrac{10}{19} = \dfrac{}{190} = \dfrac{}{95}$

218. $\dfrac{11}{15} = \dfrac{}{30} = \dfrac{55}{}$

219. $\dfrac{1}{4} = \dfrac{3}{} = \dfrac{10}{}$

220. $\dfrac{8}{10} = \dfrac{40}{} = \dfrac{64}{}$

221. $\dfrac{3}{5} = \dfrac{}{20} = \dfrac{24}{}$

222. $\dfrac{5}{6} = \dfrac{}{48} = \dfrac{45}{}$

223. $\dfrac{2}{9} = \dfrac{8}{} = \dfrac{10}{}$

224. $\dfrac{1}{3} = \dfrac{4}{} = \dfrac{5}{}$

225. $\dfrac{14}{16} = \dfrac{56}{} = \dfrac{}{32}$

226. $\dfrac{6}{11} = \dfrac{}{44} = \dfrac{60}{}$

227. $\dfrac{17}{19} = \dfrac{}{76} = \dfrac{153}{}$

228. $\dfrac{1}{2} = \dfrac{8}{} = \dfrac{}{8}$

229. $\dfrac{3}{14} = \dfrac{30}{} = \dfrac{}{98}$

230. $\dfrac{6}{8} = \dfrac{}{64} = \dfrac{12}{}$

231. $\dfrac{7}{12} = \dfrac{}{48} = \dfrac{14}{}$

232. $\dfrac{1}{13} = \dfrac{10}{} = \dfrac{6}{}$

233. $\dfrac{7}{15} = \dfrac{}{150} = \dfrac{21}{}$

234. $\dfrac{4}{17} = \dfrac{}{51} = \dfrac{20}{}$

235. $\dfrac{3}{7} = \dfrac{}{42} = \dfrac{}{49}$

236. $\dfrac{7}{18} = \dfrac{42}{} = \dfrac{}{90}$

237. $\dfrac{12}{20} = \dfrac{36}{} = \dfrac{60}{}$

238. $\dfrac{1}{3} = \dfrac{}{6} = \dfrac{}{30}$

239. $\dfrac{2}{7} = \dfrac{12}{} = \dfrac{14}{}$

240. $\dfrac{7}{9} = \dfrac{42}{} = \dfrac{}{90}$

241. $\dfrac{2}{4} = \dfrac{}{28} = \dfrac{10}{}$

242. $\dfrac{15}{20} = \dfrac{120}{} = \dfrac{30}{}$

243. $\dfrac{5}{13} = \dfrac{}{65} = \dfrac{}{117}$

244. $\dfrac{1}{12} = \dfrac{}{36} = \dfrac{8}{}$

245. $\dfrac{12}{14} = \dfrac{108}{} = \dfrac{72}{}$

246. $\dfrac{3}{5} = \dfrac{21}{} = \dfrac{}{20}$

247. $\dfrac{10}{16} = \dfrac{50}{} = \dfrac{}{64}$

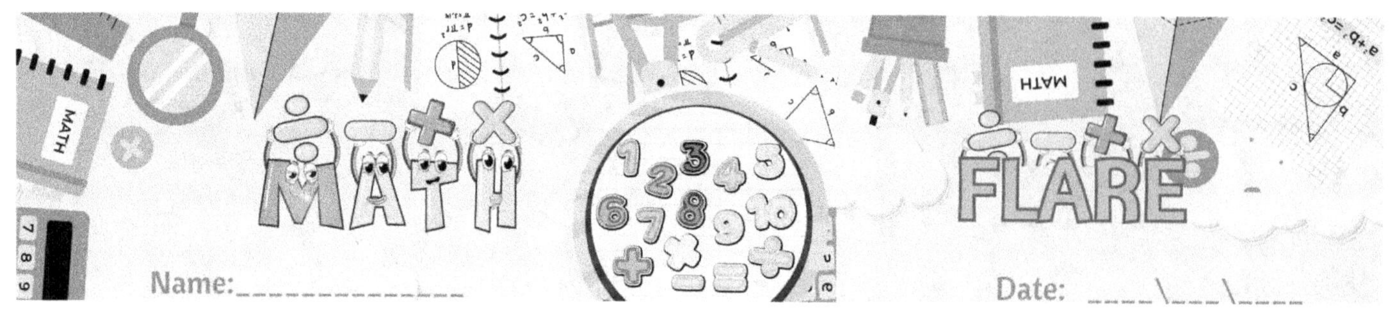

248. $\dfrac{5}{6} = \dfrac{40}{} = \dfrac{}{18}$

249. $\dfrac{1}{8} = \dfrac{}{80} = \dfrac{3}{}$

250. $\dfrac{13}{15} = \dfrac{}{60} = \dfrac{}{150}$

251. $\dfrac{8}{18} = \dfrac{80}{} = \dfrac{}{144}$

252. $\dfrac{9}{11} = \dfrac{}{66} = \dfrac{90}{}$

253. $\dfrac{12}{19} = \dfrac{}{152} = \dfrac{}{190}$

254. $\dfrac{6}{10} = \dfrac{}{90} = \dfrac{}{80}$

255. $\dfrac{13}{17} = \dfrac{}{68} = \dfrac{}{34}$

256. $\dfrac{1}{2} = \dfrac{3}{} = \dfrac{}{4}$

257. $\dfrac{12}{16} = \dfrac{}{96} = \dfrac{48}{}$

258. $\dfrac{3}{14} = \dfrac{}{140} = \dfrac{}{112}$

259. $\dfrac{2}{3} = \dfrac{}{21} = \dfrac{}{9}$

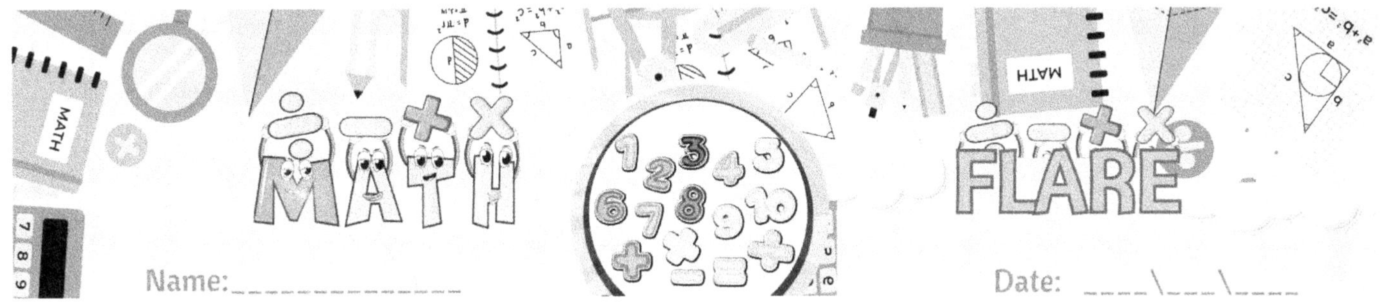

Name:_______________   Date: _____ _____ _____

Fractions Addition: Uncommon Denominator

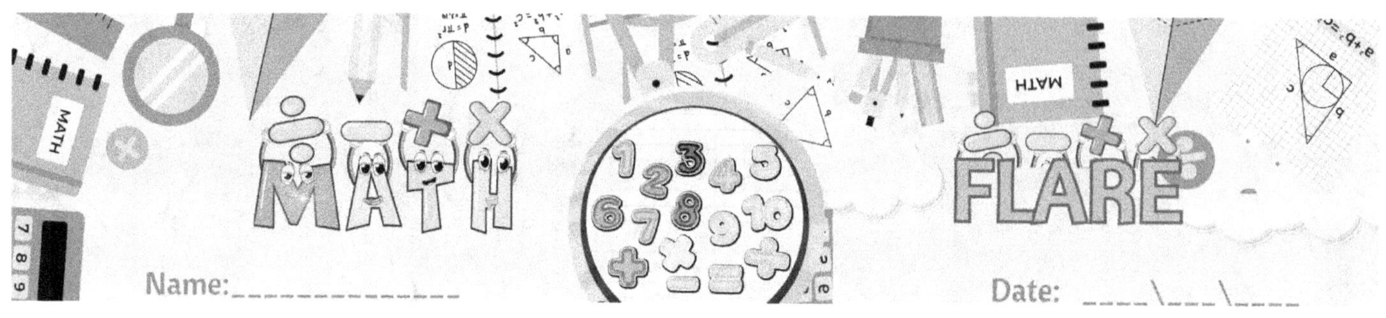

272. $\dfrac{3}{6} + \dfrac{1}{5} =$ _______________

273. $\dfrac{11}{18} + \dfrac{2}{9} =$ _______________

274. $\dfrac{1}{19} + \dfrac{9}{17} =$ _______________

275. $\dfrac{4}{10} + \dfrac{5}{12} =$ _______________

276. $\dfrac{4}{8} + \dfrac{3}{11} =$ _______________

277. $\dfrac{4}{7} + \dfrac{5}{14} =$ _______________

278. $\dfrac{2}{6} + \dfrac{4}{10} =$ _______________

279. $\dfrac{8}{20} + \dfrac{1}{3} =$ _______________

280. $\dfrac{4}{14} + \dfrac{3}{11} =$ _______________

281. $\dfrac{1}{2} + \dfrac{6}{15} =$ _______________

282. $\dfrac{1}{11} + \dfrac{18}{20} =$ _______________

283. $\dfrac{2}{17} + \dfrac{7}{9} =$ _______________

284. $\dfrac{3}{13} + \dfrac{3}{6} =$ _______________

285. $\dfrac{7}{19} + \dfrac{2}{7} =$ _______________

Name:_________________________   Date: ____________

286. $\dfrac{2}{5} + \dfrac{4}{17} =$ _______________

287. $\dfrac{4}{7} + \dfrac{6}{17} =$ _______________

288. $\dfrac{5}{17} + \dfrac{2}{13} =$ _______________

289. $\dfrac{1}{2} + \dfrac{3}{7} =$ _______________

290. $\dfrac{1}{6} + \dfrac{9}{16} =$ _______________

291. $\dfrac{8}{13} + \dfrac{3}{12} =$ _______________

292. $\dfrac{2}{3} + \dfrac{1}{9} =$ _______________

293. $\dfrac{2}{4} + \dfrac{1}{6} =$ _______________

294. $\dfrac{1}{5} + \dfrac{2}{5} =$ _______________

295. $\dfrac{9}{14} + \dfrac{4}{18} =$ _______________

296. $\dfrac{2}{10} + \dfrac{1}{3} =$ _______________

297. $\dfrac{2}{17} + \dfrac{2}{6} =$ _______________

298. $\dfrac{2}{13} + \dfrac{10}{13} =$ _______________

299. $\dfrac{4}{11} + \dfrac{3}{16} =$ _______________

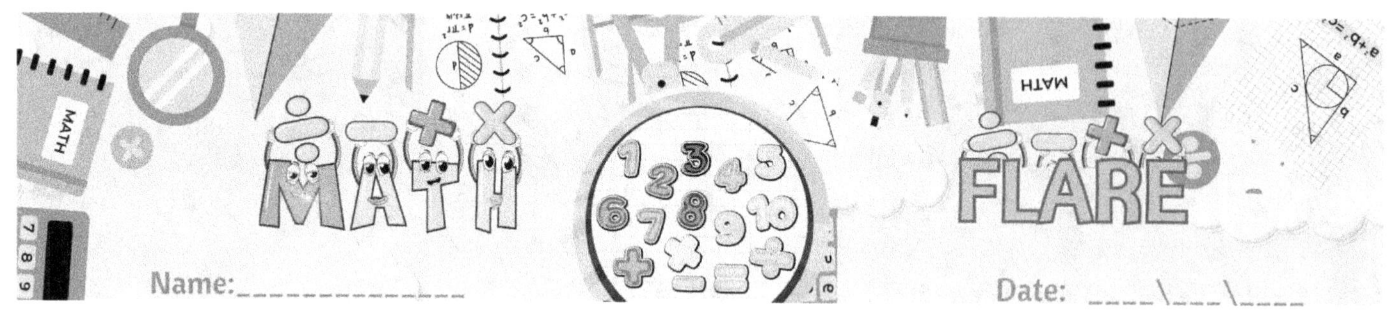

300. $\frac{1}{4} + \frac{2}{11} =$ _______________

301. $\frac{1}{10} + \frac{7}{9} =$ _______________

302. $\frac{1}{5} + \frac{10}{14} =$ _______________

303. $\frac{8}{18} + \frac{2}{5} =$ _______________

304. $\frac{1}{3} + \frac{4}{7} =$ _______________

305. $\frac{2}{20} + \frac{3}{4} =$ _______________

306. $\frac{1}{7} + \frac{2}{4} =$ _______________

307. $\frac{3}{15} + \frac{11}{15} =$ _______________

308. $\frac{7}{12} + \frac{1}{6} =$ _______________

309. $\frac{2}{8} + \frac{8}{20} =$ _______________

310. $\frac{9}{16} + \frac{5}{12} =$ _______________

311. $\frac{2}{3} + \frac{4}{13} =$ _______________

312. $\frac{6}{17} + \frac{7}{14} =$ _______________

313. $\frac{9}{10} + \frac{1}{11} =$ _______________

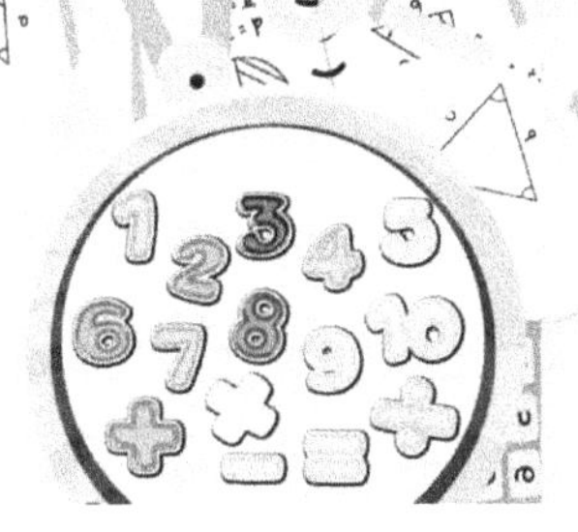

Name:____________________   Date: ____________

314. $\dfrac{2}{4} + \dfrac{3}{9} =$ _______________

315. $\dfrac{1}{2} + \dfrac{1}{7} =$ _______________

316. $\dfrac{3}{17} + \dfrac{4}{12} =$ _______________

317. $\dfrac{13}{20} + \dfrac{1}{15} =$ _______________

318. $\dfrac{3}{6} + \dfrac{1}{4} =$ _______________

319. $\dfrac{1}{14} + \dfrac{12}{14} =$ _______________

320. $\dfrac{4}{13} + \dfrac{3}{6} =$ _______________

321. $\dfrac{5}{8} + \dfrac{3}{18} =$ _______________

322. $\dfrac{1}{16} + \dfrac{7}{16} =$ _______________

323. $\dfrac{4}{12} + \dfrac{2}{8} =$ _______________

324. $\dfrac{1}{3} + \dfrac{3}{18} =$ _______________

325. $\dfrac{1}{2} + \dfrac{4}{12} =$ _______________

326. $\dfrac{2}{13} + \dfrac{3}{7} =$ _______________

327. $\dfrac{3}{7} + \dfrac{1}{2} =$ _______________

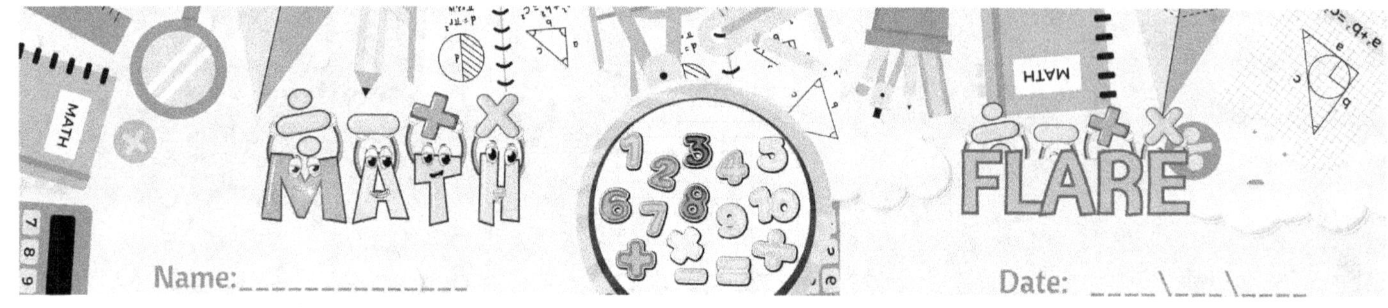

Fractions Subtraction - Uncommon Denominator

Find the difference.

328. $\dfrac{1}{2} - \dfrac{5}{11} =$ _______________

329. $\dfrac{3}{8} - \dfrac{1}{6} =$ _______________

330. $\dfrac{2}{3} - \dfrac{1}{2} =$ _______________

331. $\dfrac{4}{6} - \dfrac{5}{12} =$ _______________

332. $\dfrac{8}{10} - \dfrac{6}{9} =$ _______________

333. $\dfrac{6}{17} - \dfrac{1}{11} =$ _______________

334. $\dfrac{3}{14} - \dfrac{1}{10} =$ _______________

335. $\dfrac{6}{7} - \dfrac{1}{5} =$ _______________

336. $\dfrac{16}{19} - \dfrac{2}{10} =$ _______________

337. $\dfrac{17}{18} - \dfrac{1}{2} =$ _______________

Name:_________________   Date: ____________

338. $\dfrac{5}{9} - \dfrac{1}{3} =$ _________________

339. $\dfrac{1}{3} - \dfrac{1}{15} =$ _________________

340. $\dfrac{4}{5} - \dfrac{13}{19} =$ _________________

341. $\dfrac{10}{13} - \dfrac{1}{4} =$ _________________

342. $\dfrac{2}{3} - \dfrac{2}{5} =$ _________________

343. $\dfrac{17}{19} - \dfrac{5}{18} =$ _________________

344. $\dfrac{5}{8} - \dfrac{7}{12} =$ _________________

345. $\dfrac{4}{7} - \dfrac{1}{16} =$ _________________

346. $\dfrac{10}{20} - \dfrac{4}{17} =$ _________________

347. $\dfrac{6}{14} - \dfrac{3}{8} =$ _________________

348. $\dfrac{5}{8} - \dfrac{3}{6} =$ _________________

349. $\dfrac{4}{5} - \dfrac{3}{9} =$ _________________

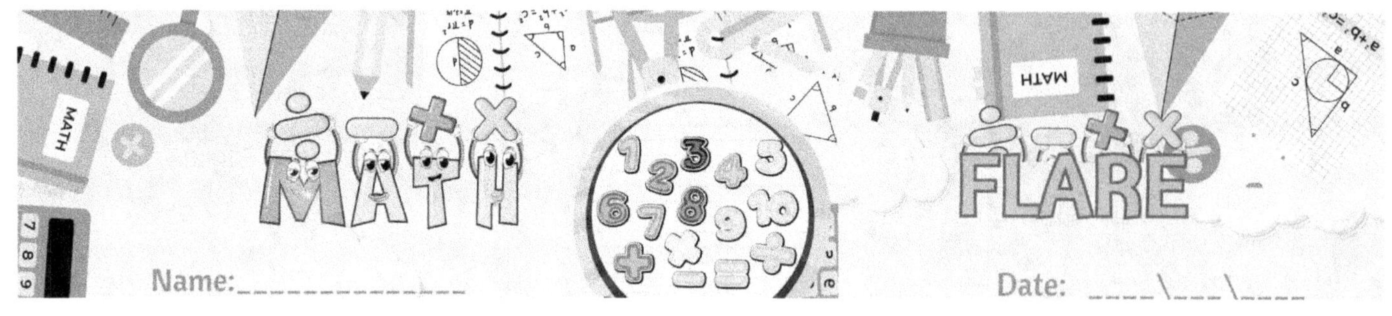

350. $\dfrac{5}{11} - \dfrac{1}{4} =$ _______________

351. $\dfrac{4}{7} - \dfrac{2}{5} =$ _______________

352. $\dfrac{7}{10} - \dfrac{2}{3} =$ _______________

353. $\dfrac{9}{19} - \dfrac{4}{10} =$ _______________

354. $\dfrac{6}{12} - \dfrac{6}{16} =$ _______________

355. $\dfrac{6}{8} - \dfrac{1}{3} =$ _______________

356. $\dfrac{16}{18} - \dfrac{1}{13} =$ _______________

357. $\dfrac{6}{9} - \dfrac{7}{14} =$ _______________

358. $\dfrac{2}{6} - \dfrac{1}{4} =$ _______________

359. $\dfrac{13}{15} - \dfrac{9}{18} =$ _______________

360. $\dfrac{2}{3} - \dfrac{5}{10} =$ _______________

361. $\dfrac{16}{17} - \dfrac{10}{13} =$ _______________

Name:________________________   Date: _______________

362. $\dfrac{1}{2} - \dfrac{2}{6} =$ ______________

363. $\dfrac{11}{19} - \dfrac{6}{16} =$ ______________

364. $\dfrac{7}{8} - \dfrac{2}{11} =$ ______________

365. $\dfrac{4}{5} - \dfrac{1}{4} =$ ______________

366. $\dfrac{3}{8} - \dfrac{2}{14} =$ ______________

367. $\dfrac{5}{6} - \dfrac{3}{8} =$ ______________

368. $\dfrac{15}{17} - \dfrac{8}{10} =$ ______________

369. $\dfrac{1}{2} - \dfrac{7}{16} =$ ______________

370. $\dfrac{5}{10} - \dfrac{1}{3} =$ ______________

371. $\dfrac{16}{18} - \dfrac{7}{11} =$ ______________

372. $\dfrac{8}{15} - \dfrac{1}{2} =$ ______________

373. $\dfrac{8}{16} - \dfrac{1}{3} =$ ______________

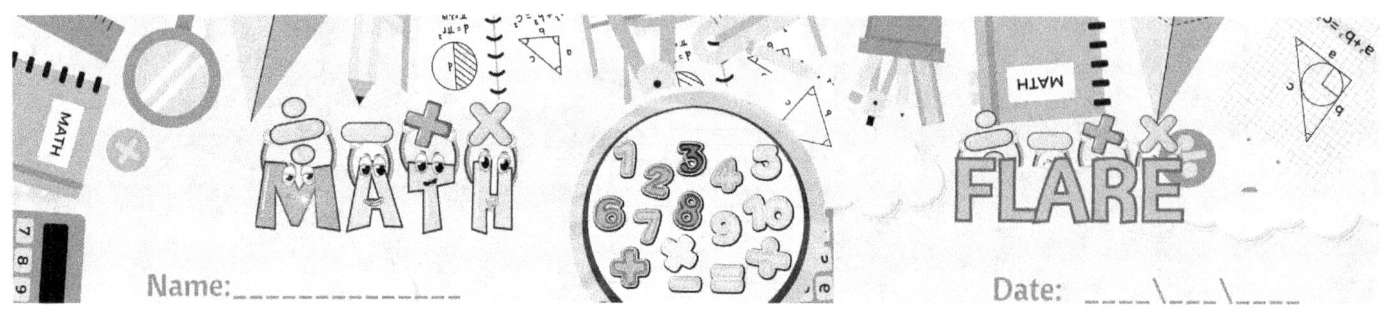

374. $\dfrac{7}{13} - \dfrac{3}{11} =$ _______________

375. $\dfrac{8}{11} - \dfrac{5}{16} =$ _______________

376. $\dfrac{3}{9} - \dfrac{2}{12} =$ _______________

377. $\dfrac{5}{6} - \dfrac{4}{20} =$ _______________

378. $\dfrac{7}{9} - \dfrac{6}{14} =$ _______________

379. $\dfrac{12}{17} - \dfrac{2}{3} =$ _______________

380. $\dfrac{5}{11} - \dfrac{4}{12} =$ _______________

381. $\dfrac{12}{18} - \dfrac{3}{5} =$ _______________

382. $\dfrac{12}{13} - \dfrac{11}{13} =$ _______________

383. $\dfrac{15}{18} - \dfrac{6}{17} =$ _______________

384. $\dfrac{5}{7} - \dfrac{4}{6} =$ _______________

385. $\dfrac{8}{11} - \dfrac{5}{7} =$ _______________

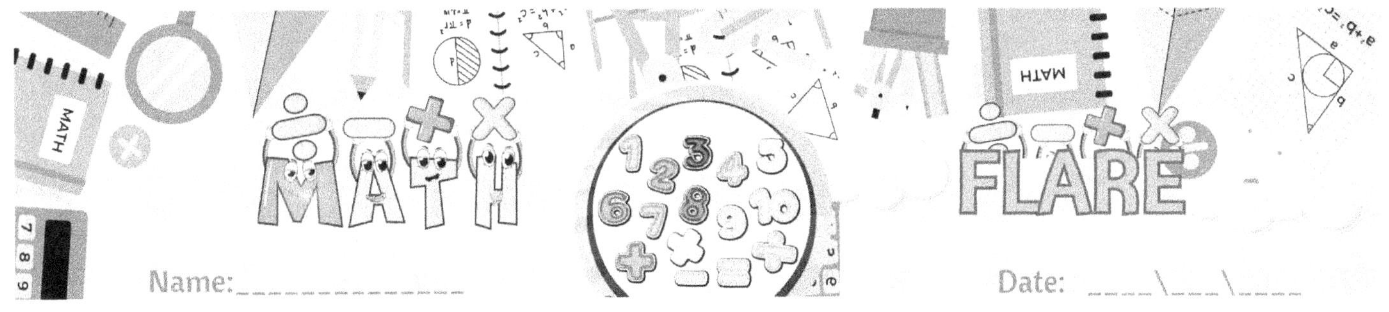

Fractions Addition Word Problems

386. A recipe calls for $\frac{1}{4}$ cups of sugar and $\frac{1}{2}$ cups of flour. How much of the mixture is needed in total?

387. Elijah drank $\frac{3}{10}$ of a bottle of water and then drank another $\frac{5}{10}$ of the bottle later. How much of the bottle did he drink in total?

388. A car travels $\frac{3}{9}$ of a mile at a constant speed and then travels another $\frac{6}{8}$ of a mile at a different constant speed. How far did the car travel in total?

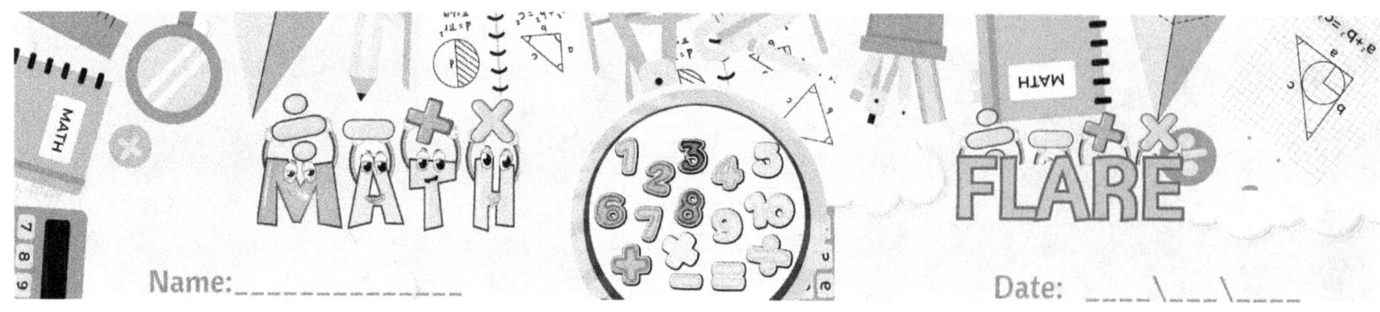

389. Noah completed $\frac{5}{7}$ of his homework and then $\frac{1}{2}$ more. How much of his homework is completed?

390. Penelope used $\frac{9}{10}$ of a stick of butter in a recipe and then used another $\frac{2}{5}$ of the stick in a different recipe. How much of the stick did she use in total?

391. Cooper ran $\frac{1}{2}$ of a mile and then walked another $\frac{2}{6}$ of a mile. How far did he travel in total?

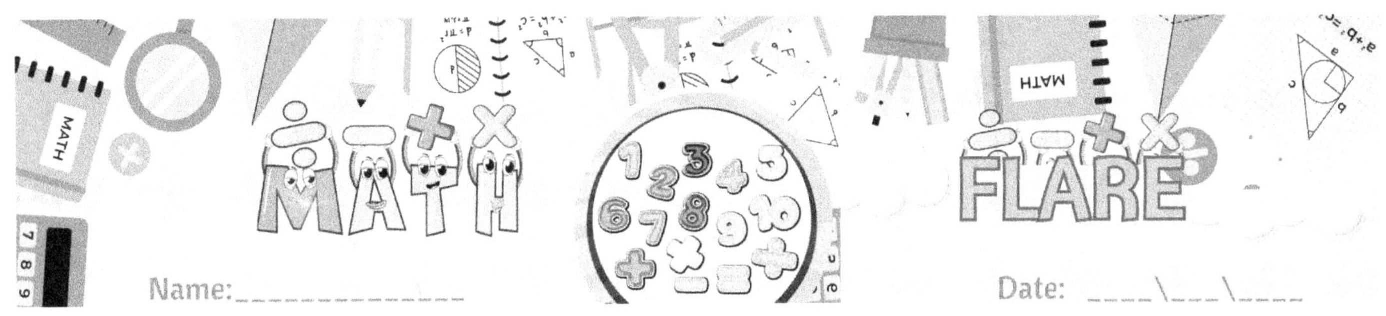

392. Harper spent $\frac{5}{6}$ of her savings on bananas and then $\frac{8}{10}$ of the remaining money on food. How much money did she spend?

393. A recipe calls for $\frac{1}{5}$ cups of strawberries and $\frac{2}{10}$ cups of bananas. How much fruit is needed in total for the recipe?

394. Naomi made a salad with $\frac{1}{2}$ of a cup of lettuce and $\frac{1}{2}$ of a cup of spinach. How much salad did she make in total?

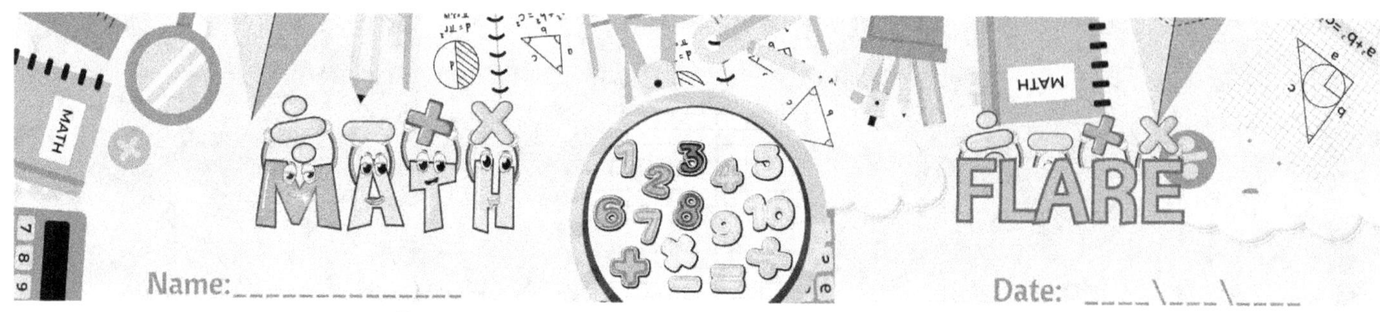

395. Henry swam $\frac{5}{7}$ of a lap and then floated another $\frac{6}{8}$ of a lap. How far did he travel in total?

396. Grace spent $\frac{2}{3}$ of her salary on spoons and then $\frac{1}{4}$ of the money on food. How much money did she spend?

397. A snack mix recipe calls for $\frac{3}{10}$ cups of almonds and $\frac{3}{9}$ cups of peanuts. How much snack mix is needed in total?

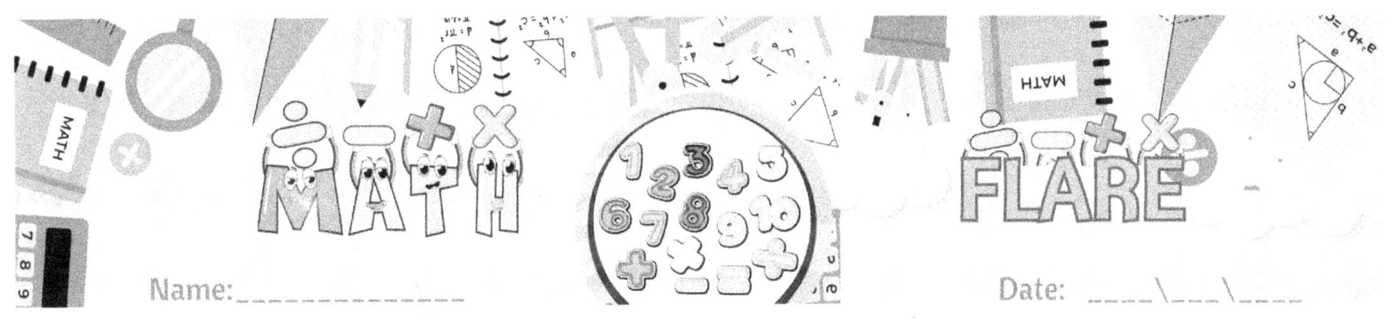

Name:_______________________   Date: ______________

398. Bella finished $\frac{7}{10}$ of a book and then read $\frac{1}{3}$ of the remaining pages. How much of the book has she read?

399. What is $\frac{2}{4}$ plus $\frac{1}{8}$?

400. Isaac paints $\frac{1}{2}$ of his paintnig on Monday, and $\frac{3}{7}$ on Tuesday. How much of his painting has he finished in total?

401. Mia cycled $\frac{4}{5}$ miles. She then stopped to buy some groceries. Then she cycled $\frac{1}{2}$ more miles. How far did Mia cycle in total?

402. If the sum of two fractions is $\frac{2}{3}$ and the first fraction is $\frac{1}{2}$, what is the second fraction?

403. Nolan jogged $\frac{1}{9}$ of a mile in the morning and then jogged another $\frac{4}{10}$ of a mile in the evening. How much did he jog in total?

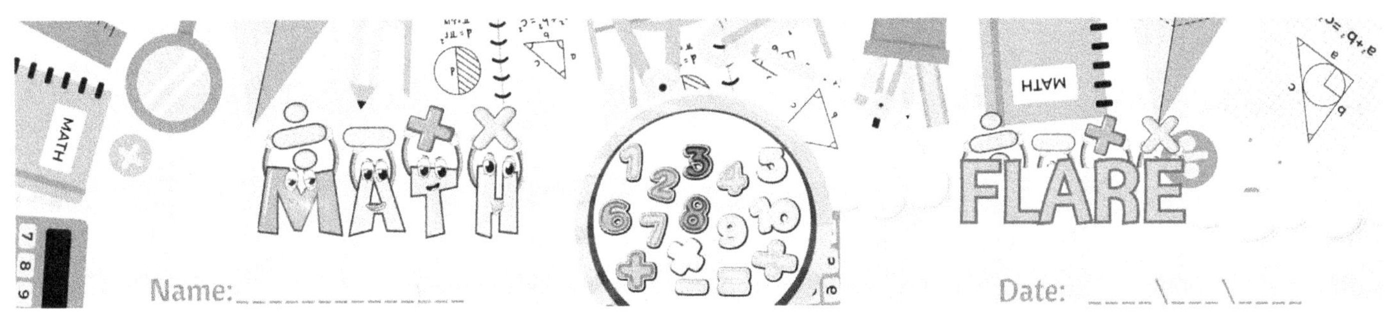

Name:_______________   Date: ___________

404. Sadie read $\frac{1}{3}$ pages of her book before bed. She then read another $\frac{2}{9}$ pages before falling asleep. How much of her book did she read in total?

405. Lucas swam $\frac{1}{4}$ of a lap in the morning and then swam another $\frac{1}{8}$ of a lap in the afternoon. How much of a lap did he swim in total?

406. Matthew ate $\frac{3}{6}$ of his pizza for dinner and then ate $\frac{3}{6}$ of the leftovers for lunch the next day. How much of his pizza did he eat in total?

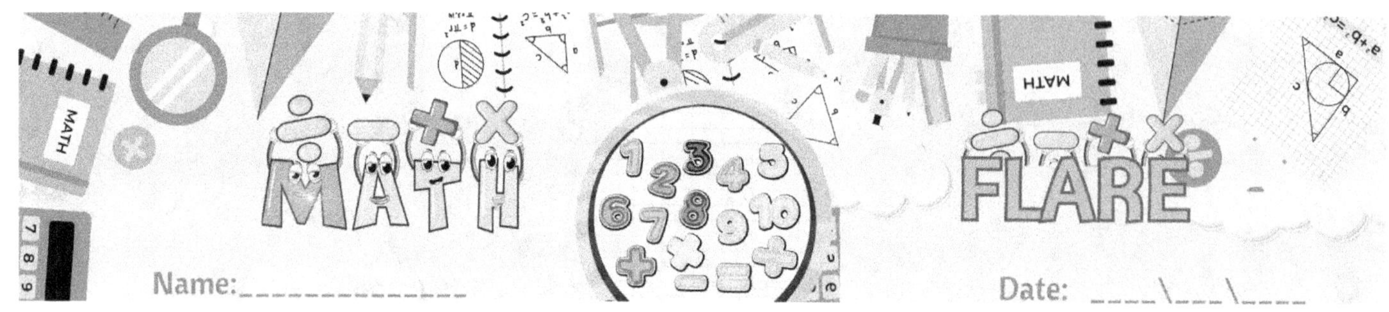

Fractions Subtraction Word Problems

407. Luna needs $\frac{2}{3}$ of a pound of cheese to make pizza. She only has $\frac{1}{2}$ of a pound of cheese. How much more cheese does she need to buy?

408. Addison is running on a track that is $\frac{3}{4}$ of a mile long. She has already run $\frac{1}{9}$ of the mile. How much further does she have to run?

409. Genesis had a cake that weighed $\frac{2}{10}$ of a pound. She cut off $\frac{1}{10}$ of a pound to share with her friends. How much cake does she have left?

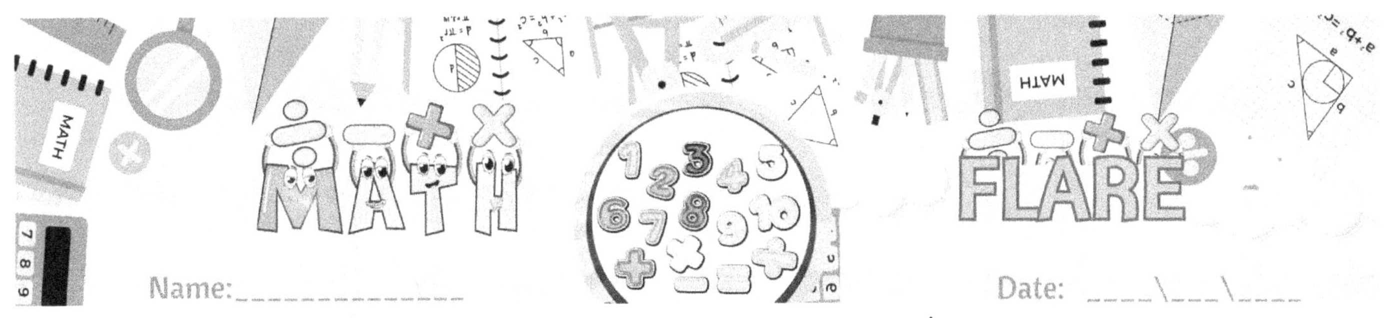

Name:_______________   Date: _______________

410. Stella has $\frac{4}{6}$ of a pound of beef. She cooks $\frac{1}{2}$ of the beef. How much beef is left in pounds?

411. Landon has a rope that is $\frac{4}{6}$ of a meter long. He needs to cut off $\frac{1}{2}$ of a meter to tie a knot. How long is the rope after the knot is tied?

412. Hailey has $\frac{1}{2}$ of a pound of flour. She uses $\frac{1}{10}$ of the flour to make a pencake. How much flour is left in pounds?

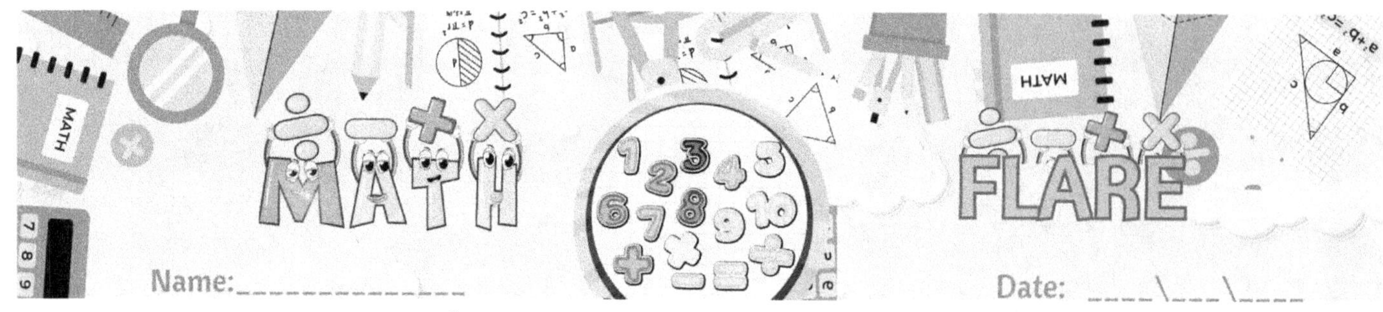

413. Reagan bought $\frac{6}{7}$ of a pound of peanuts. After sharing $\frac{4}{9}$ of the peanuts with her friend, how many pounds of peanuts did Reagan have left?

414. A recipe calls for $\frac{5}{8}$ of a cup of milk. If $\frac{2}{4}$ of the milk is already used, how much milk is left in cups?

415. Lucas has $\frac{8}{10}$ of a bag of calculators. He takes out $\frac{1}{3}$ of the calculators. How many calculators are in the bag now?

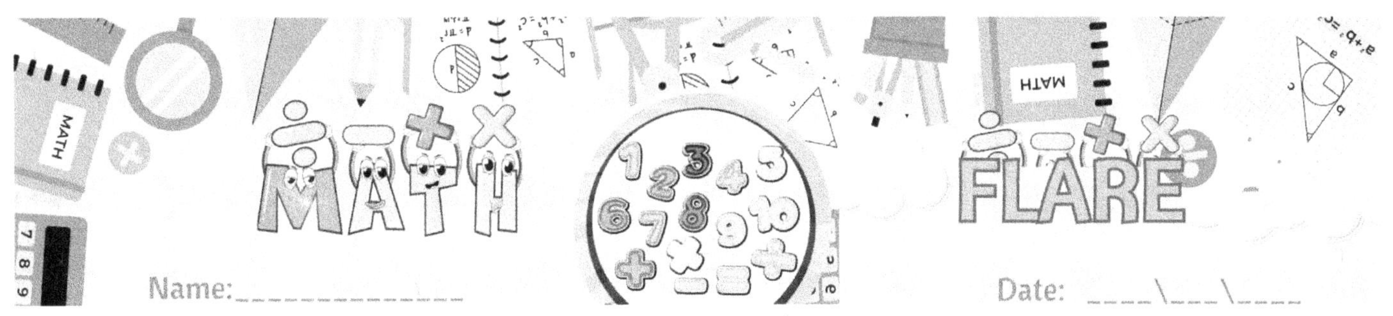

416. Alice is knitting a scarf that needs $\frac{1}{2}$ of the yarn. If she has already used $\frac{2}{3}$ yards of yarn, how much does she have left?

417. Mila is making a sweet dish and needs $\frac{3}{5}$ of a cup of strawberries. She has already used $\frac{3}{9}$ of a cup. How much more strawberry does she need?

418. Dominic has a board that is $\frac{2}{4}$ feet long. He wants to cut off $\frac{4}{10}$ of the board. How long will the board be after the cut?

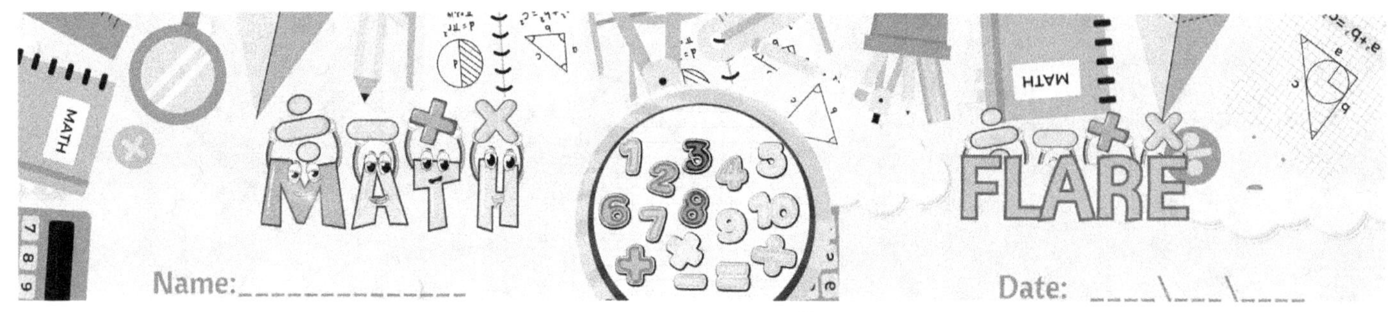

419. Anthony filled his water bottle with $\frac{3}{5}$ of a liter of water before going for a walk. During the walk, he drank $\frac{2}{9}$ of the water. How much water does he have left in the bottle?

420. Liam has $\frac{8}{10}$ of a pound of cheese. He uses $\frac{2}{5}$ of the cheese to make a sandwich. How much cheese is left in pounds?

421. Ariana needs $\frac{5}{7}$ of a cup of sugar to make lemonade. She only has $\frac{5}{9}$ of a cup of sugar. How much more sugar does she need to make the lemonade?

422. Violet wants to make a dish that calls for $\frac{1}{2}$ of a cup of yogurt. She only has $\frac{2}{10}$ of a cup of yogurt left. How much more yogurt does she need to make the dish?

423. Parker has a rope that is $\frac{7}{9}$ of a foot long. He cuts $\frac{2}{8}$ of the rope. How long is the remaining rope in feet?

424. Evan and Jordyn are cooking dinner and need $\frac{2}{3}$ of a cup of oil. Evan accidentally spills $\frac{3}{8}$ of a cup of oil. How much oil do they have left?

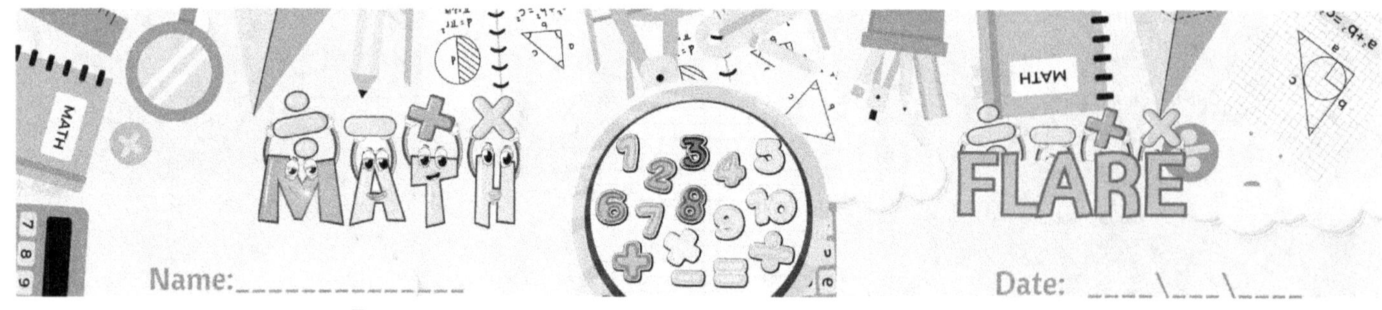

425. Lillian has $\frac{3}{4}$ of a pound of ground chicken. She uses $\frac{2}{8}$ of the chicken to make a burger. How much chicken is left in pounds?

426. Sebastian has a length of ribbon that is $\frac{6}{9}$ meters long. He wants to cut off $\frac{2}{5}$ of the ribbon to use for a gift. How long will the remaining ribbon be?

427. Xavier has $\frac{1}{9}$ of a pizza left over from last night. He eats $\frac{1}{10}$ of the pizza for lunch. How much pizza does he have left?

Name:________________ Date: ___________

Fractions Multiplication Word Problems

428. James is baking a cake that requires $\frac{1}{2}$ cup of flour. If he wants to make 4 times as much cake , how much flour does he need?

429. Roman walked $\frac{1}{3}$ of a mile every day for 7 days. How many miles did he walk in total?

430. If a garden has an area of $\frac{3}{4}$ square feet and you want to increase it by a factor of 2, what will be the new area of the garden?

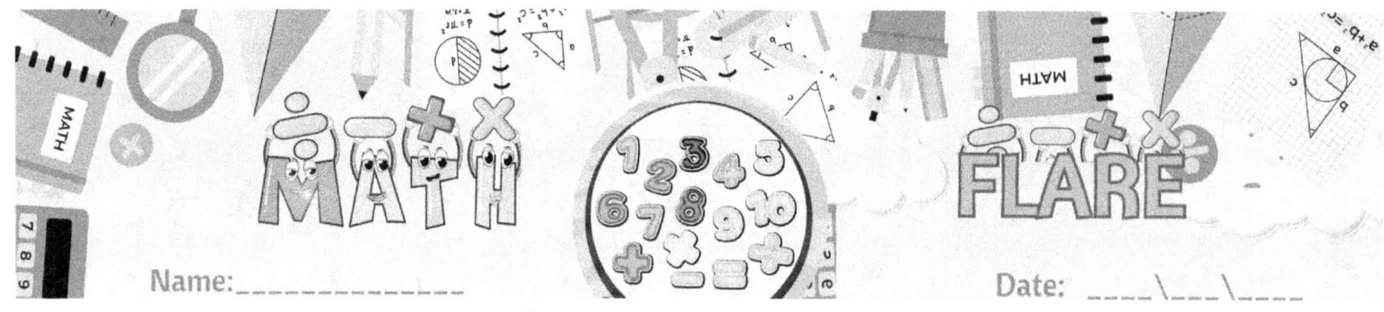

431. If a container holds $\frac{1}{8}$ of a gallon of water and you need 3 gallons of water, how many containers do you need?

432. If a person can run at a speed of $\frac{2}{3}$ miles per hour, how long will it take him to run 4 miles?

433. A basketball team wins $\frac{2}{7}$ of their games. If they play 10 games in a season, how many games did they win?

434. If a car can travel $\frac{8}{9}$ of a mile on one gallon of gas, how many miles can it travel on 3 gallons of gas?

435. If you need to make 5 batches of cookies, and each batch requires $\frac{3}{5}$ cup of chocolate chips, how many cups of chocolate chips do you need in total?

436. Brody is making a dish that calls for $\frac{1}{2}$ cup of cooking oil. If he wants to make 2 dishes of the same recipe, how much cooking oil does he need?

437. If a bag of flour weighs $\frac{2}{4}$ of a pound and you need $\frac{4}{10}$ bags, how many pounds of flour do you need in total?

438. If a container holds $\frac{4}{9}$ of a bags of socks and you need 3 bags of socks, how many containers do you need?

439. If a recipe calls for $\frac{3}{8}$ cup of sugar to make 1 dozen cookies, how much sugar is needed to make 4 dozen cookies?

440. Lydia ran $\frac{2}{9}$ miles every day for 10 days. How many miles did she run in total?

441. If a cake recipe calls for $\frac{1}{2}$ cup of flour and you want to make 4 cakes, how much flour do you need?

442. Elena needs $\frac{4}{5}$ cup of milk to make 1 cup of coffee, how much milk is needed to make 4 cups of coffee?

443. Wyatt needs $\frac{2}{7}$ cup of flour for a recipe and he wants to make $\frac{4}{5}$ batches of the recipe, how much flour will he need in total?

444. Kinsley drove $\frac{2}{4}$ of the distance to the mall. If the distance to the mall is $\frac{1}{2}$ miles, how far did Kinsley drive?

445. If a recipe calls for $\frac{9}{10}$ cup of butter and you want to make $\frac{7}{8}$ as much, how much butter do you need?

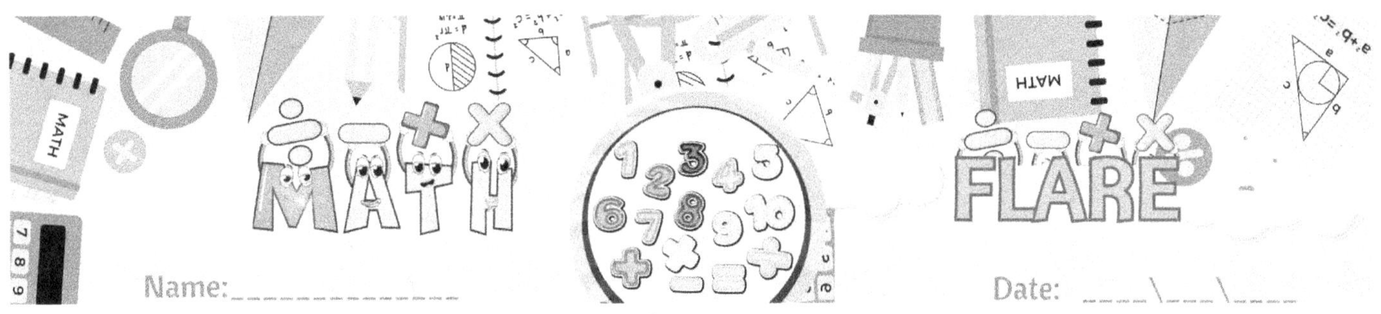

Name:_______________________   Date: ______________

446. If a company can produce $\frac{2}{5}$ of a product in one day, how many days will it take to produce 4 products?

447. A cake recipe calls for $\frac{1}{4}$ cups of sugar to make one cake. If Valentina wants to make 6 cakes, how many cups of sugar will she need?

448. If a recipe calls for $\frac{2}{4}$ cup of flour and you want to make it 5, how much flour do you need?

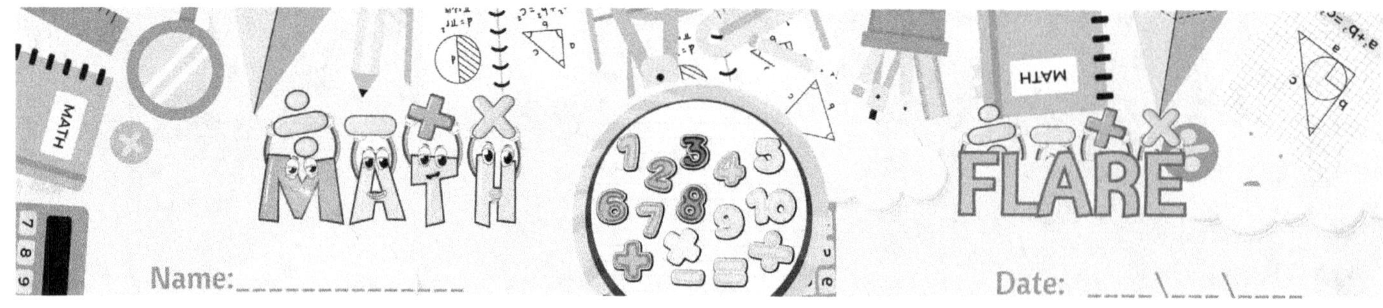

Fractions Division Word Problems

449. If you divide $\frac{5}{10}$ by $\frac{4}{10}$, what is the answer?

450. If you have $\frac{1}{9}$ of a pie and you want to share it equally with 3 friends, what fraction of the pie will each friend get?

451. If you have $\frac{3}{5}$ of a gallon of water and you want to divide it equally between 2 jugs, what fraction of a gallon of water will each jug get?

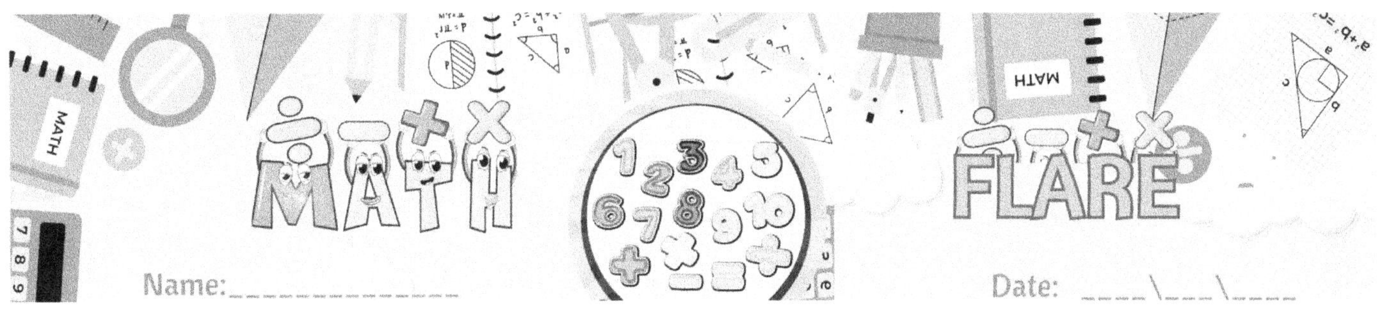

Name:______________________   Date: _______________

452. If you have $\frac{1}{2}$ of a pound of cheese and you want to divide it equally among 4 sandwiches, what fraction of a pound of cheese will each sandwich get?

453. If a bottle contains $\frac{6}{8}$ of a liter of juice and you want to split it equally between 3 people, how much juice will each person get?

454. If you have $\frac{2}{4}$ of a cup of sugar and you want to divide it equally into 2 bowls, what fraction of a cup of sugar will each bowl get?

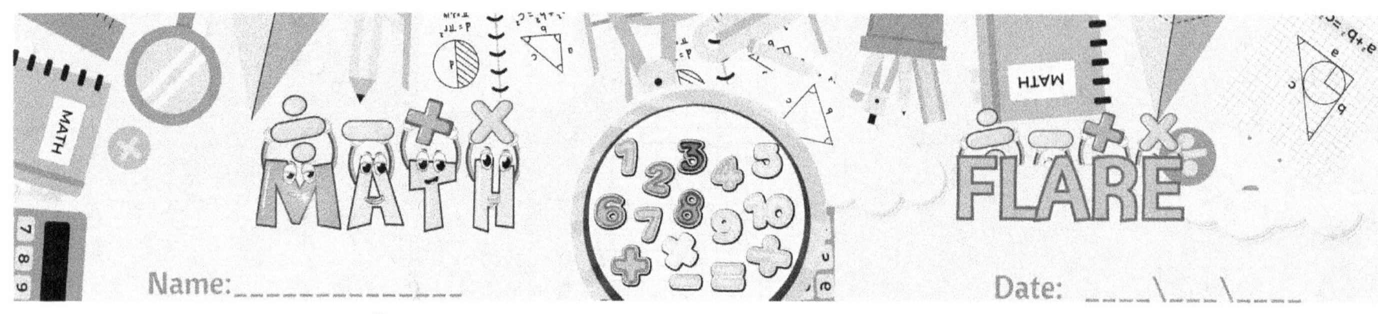

455. If you have $\frac{2}{3}$ of a cake and you want to divide it equally among 5 people, what fraction of the cake will each person get?

456. If you have $\frac{5}{6}$ of a pound of ground beef and you want to make 6 patties, how much beef is needed for each patty?

457. Peyton has $\frac{3}{7}$ of a pound of beef and she wants to divide it equally among 3 burgers, what fraction of a pound of beef will each burger get?

Name:_______________

Date: _______________

458. If a farmer has $\frac{6}{8}$ of an acre of land to plant corn, and he wants to divide the land equally into 3 parts, how much land will each part have?

459. Benjamin has $\frac{1}{5}$ of a cup of juice and he wants to divide it equally into 5 cups, what fraction of a cup of juice will each cup get?

460. If you have $\frac{2}{7}$ of a pizza and you want to share it equally with 4 friends, what fraction of the pizza will each friend get?

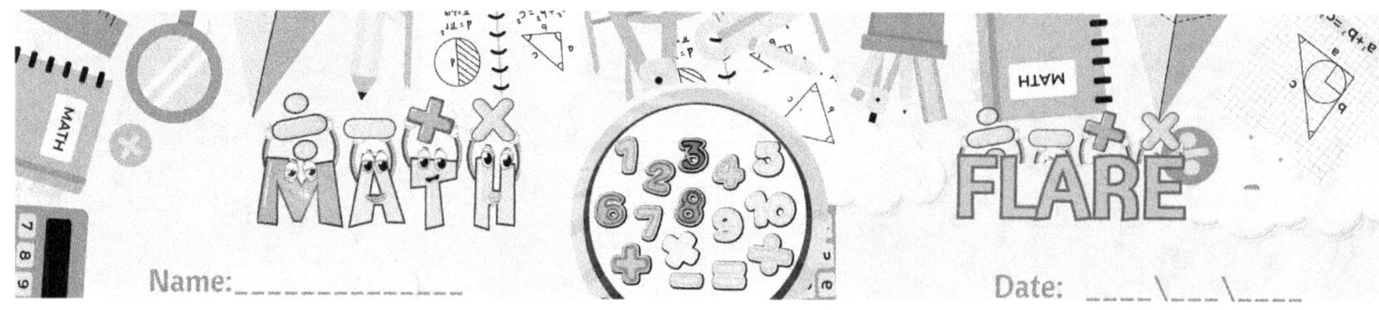

461. Naomi has $\frac{7}{10}$ of a bag of knives and she wants to divide it equally among 3 people, what fraction of the bag of knives will each person get?

462. If a bottle contains $\frac{1}{2}$ of a liter of juice and you want to split it equally between 3 people, how much juice will each person get?

463. If a farmer has $\frac{5}{6}$ of an acre of land to plant corn, and he wants to divide the land equally into 3 parts, how much land will each part have?

464. If you have $\frac{1}{3}$ of a gallon of water and you want to divide it equally among 2 jugs, what fraction of a gallon of water will each jug get?

465. Piper has $\frac{1}{9}$ of a pound of beef and she wants to divide it equally among 3 burgers, what fraction of a pound of beef will each burger get?

466. If you have $\frac{3}{4}$ of a pound of cheese and you want to divide it equally among 4 sandwiches, what fraction of a pound of cheese will each sandwich get?

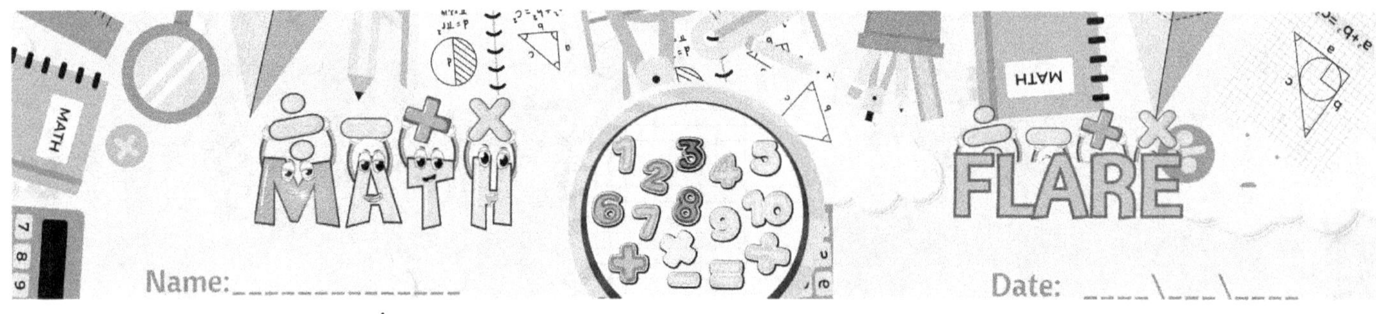

467. Landon has $\frac{1}{4}$ of a cup of juice and he wants to divide it equally into 5 cups, what fraction of a cup of juice will each cup get?

468. If you have $\frac{1}{7}$ of a cake and you want to divide it equally among 5 people, what fraction of the cake will each person get?

469. Scarlett has $\frac{3}{8}$ of a bag of clocks and she wants to divide it equally among 3 people, what fraction of the bag of clocks will each person get?

Name:_____________________   Date: ____________

Convert Fractions and Decimals

470. $\dfrac{6}{13}$ = _______________

471. 0.444 = _______________

472. 0.105 = _______________

473. $\dfrac{1}{12}$ = _______________

474. $\dfrac{4}{8}$ = _______________

475. $\dfrac{2}{7}$ = _______________

476. 0.125 = _______________

477. $\dfrac{10}{20}$ = _______________

478. $\dfrac{2}{12}$ = _______________

479. 0.636 = _______________

480. 0.111 = _______________

481. 0.444 = _______________

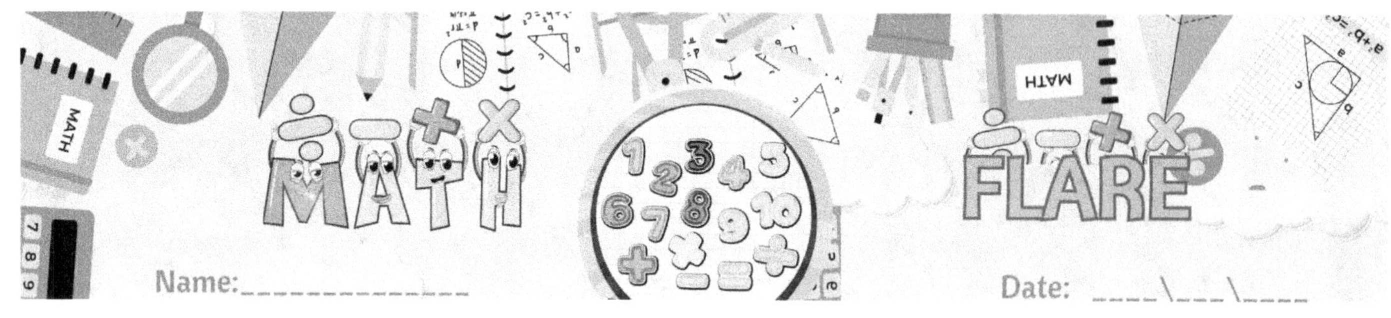

482. $0.714 =$ _______________

483. $0.25 =$ _______________

484. $0.333 =$ _______________

485. $\dfrac{1}{2} =$ _______________

486. $0.632 =$ _______________

487. $0.6 =$ _______________

488. $0.4 =$ _______________

489. $0.5 =$ _______________

490. $0.438 =$ _______________

491. $\dfrac{1}{3} =$ _______________

492. $0.077 =$ _______________

493. $\dfrac{6}{17} =$ _______________

494. $\dfrac{9}{15}$ = _______________________

495. $\dfrac{11}{12}$ = _______________________

496. 0.167 = _______________________

497. 0.714 = _______________________

498. $\dfrac{9}{10}$ = _______________________

499. 0.75 = _______________________

500. 0.071 = _______________________

501. $\dfrac{7}{20}$ = _______________________

502. 0.75 = _______________________

503. $\dfrac{10}{13}$ = _______________________

504. 0.235 = _______________________

505. 0.389 = _______________________

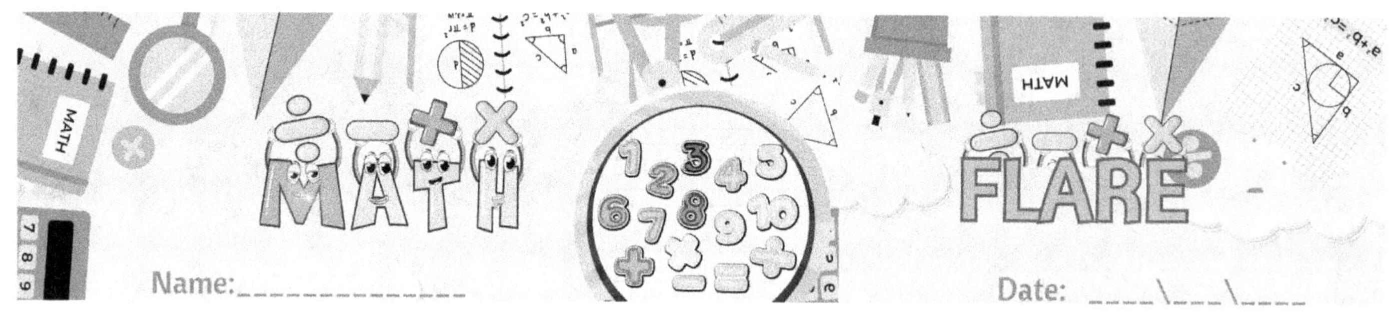

506. $0.333 =$ _______________

507. $\dfrac{3}{19} =$ _______________

508. $\dfrac{1}{16} =$ _______________

509. $0.727 =$ _______________

510. $\dfrac{4}{5} =$ _______________

511. $0.455 =$ _______________

512. $\dfrac{4}{13} =$ _______________

513. $\dfrac{5}{10} =$ _______________

514. $\dfrac{7}{14} =$ _______________

515. $0.471 =$ _______________

516. $0.474 =$ _______________

517. $\dfrac{6}{18} =$ _______________

ANSWERS

Page 1:   Adding Decimals

1. 1,062.923	2. 836.283	3. 923.894	4. 1,716.184
5. 927.296	6. 681.631	7. 832.463	8. 943.761
9. 714.646	10. 1,194.490	11. 1,227.000	12. 1,169.393
13. 563.750	14. 1,006.761	15. 1,006.825	16. 958.239
17. 862.798	18. 1,547.108	19. 990.849	20. 1,633.728
21. 526.390	22. 1,701.663	23. 859.880	24. 1,191.096
25. 1,199.344	26. 1,189.408	27. 1,479.469	28. 1,147.536
29. 653.761	30. 1,109.840	31. 957.360	32. 997.289
33. 1,081.971	34. 1,144.400	35. 702.799	36. 621.926
37. 1,070.101	38. 1,306.706	39. 878.201	40. 1,437.444
41. 1,102.955	42. 1,315.029	43. 862.663	44. 654.716
45. 1,373.290	46. 1,052.738	47. 1,750.954	48. 1,466.235
49. 1,155.339	50. 1,065.073	51. 814.543	52. 1,310.678
53. 1,198.124	54. 479.551	55. 643.155	56. 904.855
57. 1,301.510	58. 826.885	59. 1,186.780	60. 1,312.559

Page 4:   Subtracting Decimals

61. -765.265	62. 365.349	63. 688.291	64. -249.496
65. 23.587	66. 485.516	67. -105.163	68. 433.461
69. 383.146	70. 6.788	71. 354.423	72. -496.118

73. -235.820	74. 318.999	75. 270.607	76. -35.534
77. 62.401	78. -188.454	79. -204.701	80. -312.857
81. 188.769	82. 129.183	83. -139.571	84. -182.133
85. -853.248	86. -176.147	87. 171.342	88. -524.247
89. -31.726	90. 534.179	91. 142.981	92. 276.130
93. 274.417	94. 403.634	95. 212.570	96. 141.658
97. 440.033	98. -153.933	99. 58.351	100. -378.028
101. 224.401	102. -108.323	103. -460.909	104. 15.104
105. 87.992	106. -227.402	107. -50.275	108. -127.305
109. 319.053	110. -384.772	111. -563.602	112. -38.575
113. -852.472	114. -722.337	115. 225.964	116. -110.970
117. 361.156	118. -478.198	119. 820.486	120. 221.822

Page 7: Multiplying Decimals

121. 418.7568	122. 276.1838	123. 156.0230	124. 77.2048
125. 749.2608	126. 40.1617	127. 87.9504	128. 144.9140
129. 567.1800	130. 62.4874	131. 493.3214	132. 229.7868
133. 647.3328	134. 28.9280	135. 793.2731	136. 274.7256
137. 321.1546	138. 620.8635	139. 255.9522	140. 361.8357
141. 416.4880	142. 495.1296	143. 237.7680	144. 38.6207
145. 33.5570	146. 418.3740	147. 474.1152	148. 461.4400
149. 370.9804	150. 96.8000	151. 625.7170	152. 724.2228

153. 148.7912   154. 327.2220   155. 188.4251   156. 185.9760

157. 691.1820   158. 139.4752   159. 76.3421   160. 421.9033

161. 61.9029   162. 130.2846   163. 189.9597   164. 240.8400

165. 42.2586

Page 12: Dividing Decimals

166. 12.43   167. 6.24   168. 19.1   169. 19.03   170. 12.93   171. 16.13

172. 22.63   173. 16.22   174. 14.72   175. 4.11   176. 1.84   177. 19.38

178. 9.64   179. 9.73   180. 4.44   181. 2.98   182. 5.56   183. 4.2

184. 13.5   185. 1.67   186. 22.13   187. 9.33   188. 4.78   189. 19.43

190. 19.48   191. 19.3   192. 11.9   193. 10.7   194. 4.58   195. 65.2

196. 43.6   197. 10.0   198. 5.67   199. 37.85   200. 6.52   201. 4.8

Page 16: Equivalent Fractions

202. 40, 7   203. 85, 68   204. 56, 9   205. 18, 27   206. 4, 3

207. 27, 35   208. 24, 88   209. 8, 77   210. 36, 16   211. 14, 4

212. 48, 90   213. 9, 4   214. 32, 128   215. 27, 12   216. 16, 26

217. 100, 50   218. 22, 75   219. 12, 40   220. 50, 80   221. 12, 40

222. 40, 54   223. 36, 45   224. 12, 15   225. 64, 28   226. 24, 110

227. 68, 171   228. 16, 4   229. 140, 21   230. 48, 16   231. 28, 24

232. 130, 78   233. 70, 45   234. 12, 85   235. 18, 21   236. 108, 35

237. 60, 100   238. 2, 10   239. 42, 49   240. 54, 70   241. 14, 20

242. 160, 40   243. 25, 45   244. 3, 96   245. 126, 84   246. 35, 12

247. 80, 40   248. 48, 15   249. 10, 24   250. 52, 130   251. 180, 64

252. 54, 110   253. 96, 120   254. 54, 48   255. 52, 26   256. 6, 2

257. 72, 64   258. 30, 24   259. 14, 6

Page 21: Fractions Addition: Uncommon Denominator

260. 13/20   261. 5/7   262. 34/57   263. 9/20

264. 53/117   265. 185/187   266. 19/20   267. 7/9

268. 5/6   269. 7/20   270. 153/220   271. 25/68

272. 7/10   273. 5/6   274. 188/323   275. 49/60

276. 17/22   277. 13/14   278. 11/15   279. 11/15

280. 43/77   281. 9/10   282. 109/110   283. 137/153

284. 19/26   285. 87/133   286. 54/85   287. 110/119

288. 99/221   289. 13/14   290. 35/48   291. 45/52

292. 7/9   293. 2/3   294. 3/5   295. 109/126

296. 8/15   297. 23/51   298. 12/13   299. 97/176

300. 19/44   301. 79/90   302. 32/35   303. 38/45

304. 19/21   305. 17/20   306. 9/14   307. 14/15

308. 3/4   309. 13/20   310. 47/48   311. 38/39

312. 29/34   313. 109/110   314. 5/6   315. 9/14

316. 26/51   317. 43/60   318. 3/4   319. 13/14

320. 21/26   321. 19/24   322. 1/2   323. 7/12

324. 1/2   325. 5/6   326. 53/91   327. 13/14

Page 26: Fractions Subtraction - Uncommon Denominator

328. 1/22   329. 5/24   330. 1/6   331. 1/4   332. 2/15

333. 49/187   334. 4/35   335. 23/35   336. 61/95   337. 4/9

338. 2/9   339. 4/15   340. 11/95   341. 27/52   342. 4/15

343. 211/342   344. 1/24   345. 57/112   346. 9/34   347. 3/56

348. 1/8   349. 7/15   350. 9/44   351. 6/35   352. 1/30

353. 7/95   354. 1/8   355. 5/12   356. 95/117   357. 1/6

358. 1/12   359. 11/30   360. 1/6   361. 38/221   362. 1/6

363. 31/152   364. 61/88   365. 11/20   366. 13/56   367. 11/24

368. 7/85   369. 1/16   370. 1/6   371. 25/99   372. 1/30

373. 1/6   374. 38/143   375. 73/176   376. 1/6   377. 19/30

378. 22/63   379. 2/51   380. 4/33   381. 1/15   382. 1/13

383. 49/102   384. 1/21   385. 1/77

Page 31: Fractions Addition Word Problems

386. 3/4   387. 4/5   388. 1 1/12   389. 1 3/14   390. 1 3/10

391. 5/6   392. 1 19/30   393. 2/5   394. 1   395. 1 13/28

396. 11/12   397. 19/30   398. 1 1/30   399. 5/8   400. 13/14

401. 1 3/10   402. 1/6   403. 23/45   404. 5/9   405. 3/8

406. 1

Page 38: Fractions Subtraction Word Problems

407. 1/6   408. 23/36   409. 1/10   410. 1/6   411. 1/6

412. 2/5   413. 26/63   414. 1/8   415. 7/15   416. 1/6

417. 4/15   418. 1/10   419. 17/45   420. 2/5   421. 10/63

422. 3/10   423. 19/36   424. 7/24   425. 1/2   426. 4/15

427. 1/90

Page 45: Fractions Multiplication Word Problems

428. 2   429. 7/3   430. 3/2   431. 3/8   432. 8/3

433. 20/7   434. 8/3   435. 3   436. 1   437. 1/5

438. 4/3   439. 3/2   440. 20/9   441. 2   442. 16/5

443. 8/35   444. 1/4   445. 63/80   446. 8/5   447. 3/2

448. 5/2

Page 52: Fractions Division Word Problems

449. 1 1/4   450. 1/27   451. 3/10   452. 1/8   453. 1/4   454. 1/4

455. 2/15   456. 5/36   457. 1/7   458. 1/4   459. 1/25   460. 1/14

461. 7/30   462. 1/6   463. 5/18   464. 1/6   465. 1/27   466. 3/16

467. 1/20   468. 1/35   469. 1/8

Page 59: Convert Fractions and Decimals

470. 0.46   471. 4/9   472. 2/19   473. 0.08   474. 0.5   475. 0.29

476. 1/8   477. 0.5   478. 0.17   479. 7/11   480. 1/9   481. 8/18

482. 10/14   483. 1/4   484. 5/15   485. 0.5   486. 12/19   487. 3/5

488. 4/10   489. 3/6   490. 7/16   491. 0.33   492. 1/13   493. 0.35

494. 0.6   495. 0.92   496. 1/6   497. 5/7   498. 0.9   499. 3/4

500. 1/14   501. 0.35   502. 6/8   503. 0.77   504. 4/17   505. 7/18

506. 3/9   507. 0.16   508. 0.06   509. 8/11   510. 0.8   511. 5/11

512. 0.31   513. 0.5   514. 0.5   515. 8/17   516. 9/19   517. 0.33